C-1822   CAREER EXAMINATION SERIES

*This is your*
*PASSBOOK for...*

# Assistant Head Custodian

*Test Preparation Study Guide*
*Questions & Answers*

NATIONAL LEARNING CORPORATION®

# COPYRIGHT NOTICE

This book is SOLELY intended for, is sold ONLY to, and its use is RESTRICTED to individual, bona fide applicants or candidates who qualify by virtue of having seriously filed applications for appropriate license, certificate, professional and/or promotional advancement, higher school matriculation, scholarship, or other legitimate requirements of education and/or governmental authorities.

This book is NOT intended for use, class instruction, tutoring, training, duplication, copying, reprinting, excerption, or adaptation, etc., by:

1) Other publishers
2) Proprietors and/or Instructors of "Coaching" and/or Preparatory Courses
3) Personnel and/or Training Divisions of commercial, industrial, and governmental organizations
4) Schools, colleges, or universities and/or their departments and staffs, including teachers and other personnel
5) Testing Agencies or Bureaus
6) Study groups which seek by the purchase of a single volume to copy and/or duplicate and/or adapt this material for use by the group as a whole without having purchased individual volumes for each of the members of the group
7) Et al.

Such persons would be in violation of appropriate Federal and State statutes.

PROVISION OF LICENSING AGREEMENTS – Recognized educational, commercial, industrial, and governmental institutions and organizations, and others legitimately engaged in educational pursuits, including training, testing, and measurement activities, may address request for a licensing agreement to the copyright owners, who will determine whether, and under what conditions, including fees and charges, the materials in this book may be used them.  In other words, a licensing facility exists for the legitimate use of the material in this book on other than an individual basis.  However, it is asseverated and affirmed here that the material in this book CANNOT be used without the receipt of the express permission of such a licensing agreement from the Publishers.  Inquiries re licensing should be addressed to the company, attention rights and permissions department.

All rights reserved, including the right of reproduction in whole or in part, in any form or by any means, electronic or mechanical, including photocopying, recording, or by any information storage and retrieval system, without permission in writing from the Publisher.

Copyright © 2024 by
## National Learning Corporation

212 Michael Drive, Syosset, NY 11791
(516) 921-8888 • www.passbooks.com
E-mail: info@passbooks.com

PUBLISHED IN THE UNITED STATES OF AMERICA

# PASSBOOK® SERIES

THE *PASSBOOK® SERIES* has been created to prepare applicants and candidates for the ultimate academic battlefield – the examination room.

At some time in our lives, each and every one of us may be required to take an examination – for validation, matriculation, admission, qualification, registration, certification, or licensure.

Based on the assumption that every applicant or candidate has met the basic formal educational standards, has taken the required number of courses, and read the necessary texts, the *PASSBOOK® SERIES* furnishes the one special preparation which may assure passing with confidence, instead of failing with insecurity. Examination questions – together with answers – are furnished as the basic vehicle for study so that the mysteries of the examination and its compounding difficulties may be eliminated or diminished by a sure method.

This book is meant to help you pass your examination provided that you qualify and are serious in your objective.

The entire field is reviewed through the huge store of content information which is succinctly presented through a provocative and challenging approach – the question-and-answer method.

A climate of success is established by furnishing the correct answers at the end of each test.

You soon learn to recognize types of questions, forms of questions, and patterns of questioning. You may even begin to anticipate expected outcomes.

You perceive that many questions are repeated or adapted so that you can gain acute insights, which may enable you to score many sure points.

You learn how to confront new questions, or types of questions, and to attack them confidently and work out the correct answers.

You note objectives and emphases, and recognize pitfalls and dangers, so that you may make positive educational adjustments.

Moreover, you are kept fully informed in relation to new concepts, methods, practices, and directions in the field.

You discover that you are actually taking the examination all the time: you are preparing for the examination by "taking" an examination, not by reading extraneous and/or supererogatory textbooks.

In short, this PASSBOOK®, used directedly, should be an important factor in helping you to pass your test.

# ASSISTANT HEAD CUSTODIAN

## DUTIES
Performs custodial duties and supervises a crew either on a night shift or in an assigned area of a school; performs related duties as required.

## SCOPE OF THE EXAMINATION
The written test will cover knowledge, skills and/or abilities in such areas as:
1. Ability to read and follow written instructions;
2. Operation and maintenance of heating, ventilating and air conditioning systems;
3. Building cleaning;
4. Building operation and maintenance;
5. Keeping simple inventory records; and
6. Supervision and training.

# HOW TO TAKE A TEST

I. YOU MUST PASS AN EXAMINATION

A. *WHAT EVERY CANDIDATE SHOULD KNOW*

Examination applicants often ask us for help in preparing for the written test. What can I study in advance? What kinds of questions will be asked? How will the test be given? How will the papers be graded?

As an applicant for a civil service examination, you may be wondering about some of these things. Our purpose here is to suggest effective methods of advance study and to describe civil service examinations.

Your chances for success on this examination can be increased if you know how to prepare. Those "pre-examination jitters" can be reduced if you know what to expect. You can even experience an adventure in good citizenship if you know why civil service exams are given.

B. *WHY ARE CIVIL SERVICE EXAMINATIONS GIVEN?*

Civil service examinations are important to you in two ways. As a citizen, you want public jobs filled by employees who know how to do their work. As a job seeker, you want a fair chance to compete for that job on an equal footing with other candidates. The best-known means of accomplishing this two-fold goal is the competitive examination.

Exams are widely publicized throughout the nation. They may be administered for jobs in federal, state, city, municipal, town or village governments or agencies.

Any citizen may apply, with some limitations, such as the age or residence of applicants. Your experience and education may be reviewed to see whether you meet the requirements for the particular examination. When these requirements exist, they are reasonable and applied consistently to all applicants. Thus, a competitive examination may cause you some uneasiness now, but it is your privilege and safeguard.

C. *HOW ARE CIVIL SERVICE EXAMS DEVELOPED?*

Examinations are carefully written by trained technicians who are specialists in the field known as "psychological measurement," in consultation with recognized authorities in the field of work that the test will cover. These experts recommend the subject matter areas or skills to be tested; only those knowledges or skills important to your success on the job are included. The most reliable books and source materials available are used as references. Together, the experts and technicians judge the difficulty level of the questions.

Test technicians know how to phrase questions so that the problem is clearly stated. Their ethics do not permit "trick" or "catch" questions. Questions may have been tried out on sample groups, or subjected to statistical analysis, to determine their usefulness.

Written tests are often used in combination with performance tests, ratings of training and experience, and oral interviews. All of these measures combine to form the best-known means of finding the right person for the right job.

## II. HOW TO PASS THE WRITTEN TEST

### A. NATURE OF THE EXAMINATION

To prepare intelligently for civil service examinations, you should know how they differ from school examinations you have taken. In school you were assigned certain definite pages to read or subjects to cover. The examination questions were quite detailed and usually emphasized memory. Civil service exams, on the other hand, try to discover your present ability to perform the duties of a position, plus your potentiality to learn these duties. In other words, a civil service exam attempts to predict how successful you will be. Questions cover such a broad area that they cannot be as minute and detailed as school exam questions.

In the public service similar kinds of work, or positions, are grouped together in one "class." This process is known as *position-classification*. All the positions in a class are paid according to the salary range for that class. One class title covers all of these positions, and they are all tested by the same examination.

### B. FOUR BASIC STEPS

#### 1) Study the announcement

How, then, can you know what subjects to study? Our best answer is: "Learn as much as possible about the class of positions for which you've applied." The exam will test the knowledge, skills and abilities needed to do the work.

Your most valuable source of information about the position you want is the official exam announcement. This announcement lists the training and experience qualifications. Check these standards and apply only if you come reasonably close to meeting them.

The brief description of the position in the examination announcement offers some clues to the subjects which will be tested. Think about the job itself. Review the duties in your mind. Can you perform them, or are there some in which you are rusty? Fill in the blank spots in your preparation.

Many jurisdictions preview the written test in the exam announcement by including a section called "Knowledge and Abilities Required," "Scope of the Examination," or some similar heading. Here you will find out specifically what fields will be tested.

#### 2) Review your own background

Once you learn in general what the position is all about, and what you need to know to do the work, ask yourself which subjects you already know fairly well and which need improvement. You may wonder whether to concentrate on improving your strong areas or on building some background in your fields of weakness. When the announcement has specified "some knowledge" or "considerable knowledge," or has used adjectives like "beginning principles of…" or "advanced … methods," you can get a clue as to the number and difficulty of questions to be asked in any given field. More questions, and hence broader coverage, would be included for those subjects which are more important in the work. Now weigh your strengths and weaknesses against the job requirements and prepare accordingly.

#### 3) Determine the level of the position

Another way to tell how intensively you should prepare is to understand the level of the job for which you are applying. Is it the entering level? In other words, is this the position in which beginners in a field of work are hired? Or is it an intermediate or advanced level? Sometimes this is indicated by such words as "Junior" or "Senior" in the class title. Other jurisdictions use Roman numerals to designate the level – Clerk I, Clerk II, for example. The word "Supervisor" sometimes appears in the title. If the level is not indicated by the title, check the description of duties. Will you be working under very close supervision, or will you have responsibility for independent decisions in this work?

**4) Choose appropriate study materials**

Now that you know the subjects to be examined and the relative amount of each subject to be covered, you can choose suitable study materials. For beginning level jobs, or even advanced ones, if you have a pronounced weakness in some aspect of your training, read a modern, standard textbook in that field. Be sure it is up to date and has general coverage. Such books are normally available at your library, and the librarian will be glad to help you locate one. For entry-level positions, questions of appropriate difficulty are chosen – neither highly advanced questions, nor those too simple. Such questions require careful thought but not advanced training.

If the position for which you are applying is technical or advanced, you will read more advanced, specialized material. If you are already familiar with the basic principles of your field, elementary textbooks would waste your time. Concentrate on advanced textbooks and technical periodicals. Think through the concepts and review difficult problems in your field.

These are all general sources. You can get more ideas on your own initiative, following these leads. For example, training manuals and publications of the government agency which employs workers in your field can be useful, particularly for technical and professional positions. A letter or visit to the government department involved may result in more specific study suggestions, and certainly will provide you with a more definite idea of the exact nature of the position you are seeking.


III. KINDS OF TESTS

Tests are used for purposes other than measuring knowledge and ability to perform specified duties. For some positions, it is equally important to test ability to make adjustments to new situations or to profit from training. In others, basic mental abilities not dependent on information are essential. Questions which test these things may not appear as pertinent to the duties of the position as those which test for knowledge and information. Yet they are often highly important parts of a fair examination. For very general questions, it is almost impossible to help you direct your study efforts. What we can do is to point out some of the more common of these general abilities needed in public service positions and describe some typical questions.

1) General information

Broad, general information has been found useful for predicting job success in some kinds of work. This is tested in a variety of ways, from vocabulary lists to questions about current events. Basic background in some field of work, such as sociology or economics, may be sampled in a group of questions. Often these are principles which have become familiar to most persons through exposure rather than through formal training. It is difficult to advise you how to study for these questions; being alert to the world around you is our best suggestion.

2) Verbal ability

An example of an ability needed in many positions is verbal or language ability. Verbal ability is, in brief, the ability to use and understand words. Vocabulary and grammar tests are typical measures of this ability. Reading comprehension or paragraph interpretation questions are common in many kinds of civil service tests. You are given a paragraph of written material and asked to find its central meaning.

3) Numerical ability

Number skills can be tested by the familiar arithmetic problem, by checking paired lists of numbers to see which are alike and which are different, or by interpreting charts and graphs. In the latter test, a graph may be printed in the test booklet which you are asked to use as the basis for answering questions.

4) Observation

A popular test for law-enforcement positions is the observation test. A picture is shown to you for several minutes, then taken away. Questions about the picture test your ability to observe both details and larger elements.

5) Following directions

In many positions in the public service, the employee must be able to carry out written instructions dependably and accurately. You may be given a chart with several columns, each column listing a variety of information. The questions require you to carry out directions involving the information given in the chart.

6) Skills and aptitudes

Performance tests effectively measure some manual skills and aptitudes. When the skill is one in which you are trained, such as typing or shorthand, you can practice. These tests are often very much like those given in business school or high school courses. For many of the other skills and aptitudes, however, no short-time preparation can be made. Skills and abilities natural to you or that you have developed throughout your lifetime are being tested.

Many of the general questions just described provide all the data needed to answer the questions and ask you to use your reasoning ability to find the answers. Your best preparation for these tests, as well as for tests of facts and ideas, is to be at your physical and mental best. You, no doubt, have your own methods of getting into an exam-taking mood and keeping "in shape." The next section lists some ideas on this subject.

## IV. KINDS OF QUESTIONS

Only rarely is the "essay" question, which you answer in narrative form, used in civil service tests. Civil service tests are usually of the short-answer type. Full instructions for answering these questions will be given to you at the examination. But in case this is your first experience with short-answer questions and separate answer sheets, here is what you need to know:

### 1) Multiple-choice Questions

Most popular of the short-answer questions is the "multiple choice" or "best answer" question. It can be used, for example, to test for factual knowledge, ability to solve problems or judgment in meeting situations found at work.

A multiple-choice question is normally one of three types—
- It can begin with an incomplete statement followed by several possible endings. You are to find the one ending which *best* completes the statement, although some of the others may not be entirely wrong.
- It can also be a complete statement in the form of a question which is answered by choosing one of the statements listed.

- It can be in the form of a problem – again you select the best answer.

Here is an example of a multiple-choice question with a discussion which should give you some clues as to the method for choosing the right answer:

When an employee has a complaint about his assignment, the action which will *best* help him overcome his difficulty is to
  A. discuss his difficulty with his coworkers
  B. take the problem to the head of the organization
  C. take the problem to the person who gave him the assignment
  D. say nothing to anyone about his complaint

In answering this question, you should study each of the choices to find which is best. Consider choice "A" – Certainly an employee may discuss his complaint with fellow employees, but no change or improvement can result, and the complaint remains unresolved. Choice "B" is a poor choice since the head of the organization probably does not know what assignment you have been given, and taking your problem to him is known as "going over the head" of the supervisor. The supervisor, or person who made the assignment, is the person who can clarify it or correct any injustice. Choice "C" is, therefore, correct. To say nothing, as in choice "D," is unwise. Supervisors have and interest in knowing the problems employees are facing, and the employee is seeking a solution to his problem.

## 2) True/False Questions

The "true/false" or "right/wrong" form of question is sometimes used. Here a complete statement is given. Your job is to decide whether the statement is right or wrong.

SAMPLE: A roaming cell-phone call to a nearby city costs less than a non-roaming call to a distant city.

This statement is wrong, or false, since roaming calls are more expensive.
This is not a complete list of all possible question forms, although most of the others are variations of these common types. You will always get complete directions for answering questions. Be sure you understand *how* to mark your answers – ask questions until you do.


## V. RECORDING YOUR ANSWERS

Computer terminals are used more and more today for many different kinds of exams.
For an examination with very few applicants, you may be told to record your answers in the test booklet itself. Separate answer sheets are much more common. If this separate answer sheet is to be scored by machine – and this is often the case – it is highly important that you mark your answers correctly in order to get credit.
An electronic scoring machine is often used in civil service offices because of the speed with which papers can be scored. Machine-scored answer sheets must be marked with a pencil, which will be given to you. This pencil has a high graphite content which responds to the electronic scoring machine. As a matter of fact, stray dots may register as answers, so do not let your pencil rest on the answer sheet while you are pondering the correct answer. Also, if your pencil lead breaks or is otherwise defective, ask for another.

Since the answer sheet will be dropped in a slot in the scoring machine, be careful not to bend the corners or get the paper crumpled.

The answer sheet normally has five vertical columns of numbers, with 30 numbers to a column. These numbers correspond to the question numbers in your test booklet. After each number, going across the page are four or five pairs of dotted lines. These short dotted lines have small letters or numbers above them. The first two pairs may also have a "T" or "F" above the letters. This indicates that the first two pairs only are to be used if the questions are of the true-false type. If the questions are multiple choice, disregard the "T" and "F" and pay attention only to the small letters or numbers.

Answer your questions in the manner of the sample that follows:

32. The largest city in the United States is
    A. Washington, D.C.
    B. New York City
    C. Chicago
    D. Detroit
    E. San Francisco

1) Choose the answer you think is best. (New York City is the largest, so "B" is correct.)
2) Find the row of dotted lines numbered the same as the question you are answering. (Find row number 32)
3) Find the pair of dotted lines corresponding to the answer. (Find the pair of lines under the mark "B.")
4) Make a solid black mark between the dotted lines.

## VI. BEFORE THE TEST

Common sense will help you find procedures to follow to get ready for an examination. Too many of us, however, overlook these sensible measures. Indeed, nervousness and fatigue have been found to be the most serious reasons why applicants fail to do their best on civil service tests. Here is a list of reminders:

- Begin your preparation early – Don't wait until the last minute to go scurrying around for books and materials or to find out what the position is all about.
- Prepare continuously – An hour a night for a week is better than an all-night cram session. This has been definitely established. What is more, a night a week for a month will return better dividends than crowding your study into a shorter period of time.
- Locate the place of the exam – You have been sent a notice telling you when and where to report for the examination. If the location is in a different town or otherwise unfamiliar to you, it would be well to inquire the best route and learn something about the building.
- Relax the night before the test – Allow your mind to rest. Do not study at all that night. Plan some mild recreation or diversion; then go to bed early and get a good night's sleep.
- Get up early enough to make a leisurely trip to the place for the test – This way unforeseen events, traffic snarls, unfamiliar buildings, etc. will not upset you.
- Dress comfortably – A written test is not a fashion show. You will be known by number and not by name, so wear something comfortable.

- Leave excess paraphernalia at home – Shopping bags and odd bundles will get in your way. You need bring only the items mentioned in the official notice you received; usually everything you need is provided. Do not bring reference books to the exam. They will only confuse those last minutes and be taken away from you when in the test room.
- Arrive somewhat ahead of time – If because of transportation schedules you must get there very early, bring a newspaper or magazine to take your mind off yourself while waiting.
- Locate the examination room – When you have found the proper room, you will be directed to the seat or part of the room where you will sit. Sometimes you are given a sheet of instructions to read while you are waiting. Do not fill out any forms until you are told to do so; just read them and be prepared.
- Relax and prepare to listen to the instructions
- If you have any physical problem that may keep you from doing your best, be sure to tell the test administrator. If you are sick or in poor health, you really cannot do your best on the exam. You can come back and take the test some other time.

## VII. AT THE TEST

The day of the test is here and you have the test booklet in your hand. The temptation to get going is very strong. Caution! There is more to success than knowing the right answers. You must know how to identify your papers and understand variations in the type of short-answer question used in this particular examination. Follow these suggestions for maximum results from your efforts:

### 1) Cooperate with the monitor

The test administrator has a duty to create a situation in which you can be as much at ease as possible. He will give instructions, tell you when to begin, check to see that you are marking your answer sheet correctly, and so on. He is not there to guard you, although he will see that your competitors do not take unfair advantage. He wants to help you do your best.

### 2) Listen to all instructions

Don't jump the gun! Wait until you understand all directions. In most civil service tests you get more time than you need to answer the questions. So don't be in a hurry. Read each word of instructions until you clearly understand the meaning. Study the examples, listen to all announcements and follow directions. Ask questions if you do not understand what to do.

### 3) Identify your papers

Civil service exams are usually identified by number only. You will be assigned a number; you must not put your name on your test papers. Be sure to copy your number correctly. Since more than one exam may be given, copy your exact examination title.

### 4) Plan your time

Unless you are told that a test is a "speed" or "rate of work" test, speed itself is usually not important. Time enough to answer all the questions will be provided, but this does not mean that you have all day. An overall time limit has been set. Divide the total time (in minutes) by the number of questions to determine the approximate time you have for each question.

### 5) Do not linger over difficult questions

If you come across a difficult question, mark it with a paper clip (useful to have along) and come back to it when you have been through the booklet. One caution if you do this – be sure to skip a number on your answer sheet as well. Check often to be sure that you have not lost your place and that you are marking in the row numbered the same as the question you are answering.

### 6) Read the questions

Be sure you know what the question asks! Many capable people are unsuccessful because they failed to *read* the questions correctly.

### 7) Answer all questions

Unless you have been instructed that a penalty will be deducted for incorrect answers, it is better to guess than to omit a question.

### 8) Speed tests

It is often better NOT to guess on speed tests. It has been found that on timed tests people are tempted to spend the last few seconds before time is called in marking answers at random – without even reading them – in the hope of picking up a few extra points. To discourage this practice, the instructions may warn you that your score will be "corrected" for guessing. That is, a penalty will be applied. The incorrect answers will be deducted from the correct ones, or some other penalty formula will be used.

### 9) Review your answers

If you finish before time is called, go back to the questions you guessed or omitted to give them further thought. Review other answers if you have time.

### 10) Return your test materials

If you are ready to leave before others have finished or time is called, take ALL your materials to the monitor and leave quietly. Never take any test material with you. The monitor can discover whose papers are not complete, and taking a test booklet may be grounds for disqualification.

## VIII. EXAMINATION TECHNIQUES

1) Read the general instructions carefully. These are usually printed on the first page of the exam booklet. As a rule, these instructions refer to the timing of the examination; the fact that you should not start work until the signal and must stop work at a signal, etc. If there are any *special* instructions, such as a choice of questions to be answered, make sure that you note this instruction carefully.

2) When you are ready to start work on the examination, that is as soon as the signal has been given, read the instructions to each question booklet, underline any key words or phrases, such as *least, best, outline, describe* and the like. In this way you will tend to answer as requested rather than discover on reviewing your paper that you *listed without describing*, that you selected the *worst* choice rather than the *best* choice, etc.

3) If the examination is of the objective or multiple-choice type – that is, each question will also give a series of possible answers: A, B, C or D, and you are called upon to select the best answer and write the letter next to that answer on your answer paper – it is advisable to start answering each question in turn. There may be anywhere from 50 to 100 such questions in the three or four hours allotted and you can see how much time would be taken if you read through all the questions before beginning to answer any. Furthermore, if you come across a question or group of questions which you know would be difficult to answer, it would undoubtedly affect your handling of all the other questions.

4) If the examination is of the essay type and contains but a few questions, it is a moot point as to whether you should read all the questions before starting to answer any one. Of course, if you are given a choice – say five out of seven and the like – then it is essential to read all the questions so you can eliminate the two that are most difficult. If, however, you are asked to answer all the questions, there may be danger in trying to answer the easiest one first because you may find that you will spend too much time on it. The best technique is to answer the first question, then proceed to the second, etc.

5) Time your answers. Before the exam begins, write down the time it started, then add the time allowed for the examination and write down the time it must be completed, then divide the time available somewhat as follows:
    - If 3-1/2 hours are allowed, that would be 210 minutes. If you have 80 objective-type questions, that would be an average of 2-1/2 minutes per question. Allow yourself no more than 2 minutes per question, or a total of 160 minutes, which will permit about 50 minutes to review.
    - If for the time allotment of 210 minutes there are 7 essay questions to answer, that would average about 30 minutes a question. Give yourself only 25 minutes per question so that you have about 35 minutes to review.

6) The most important instruction is to *read each question* and make sure you know what is wanted. The second most important instruction is to *time yourself properly* so that you answer every question. The third most important instruction is to *answer every question*. Guess if you have to but include something for each question. Remember that you will receive no credit for a blank and will probably receive some credit if you write something in answer to an essay question. If you guess a letter – say "B" for a multiple-choice question – you may have guessed right. If you leave a blank as an answer to a multiple-choice question, the examiners may respect your feelings but it will not add a point to your score. Some exams may penalize you for wrong answers, so in such cases *only*, you may not want to guess unless you have some basis for your answer.

7) Suggestions
    a. Objective-type questions
        1. Examine the question booklet for proper sequence of pages and questions
        2. Read all instructions carefully
        3. Skip any question which seems too difficult; return to it after all other questions have been answered
        4. Apportion your time properly; do not spend too much time on any single question or group of questions

5. Note and underline key words – *all, most, fewest, least, best, worst, same, opposite*, etc.
6. Pay particular attention to negatives
7. Note unusual option, e.g., unduly long, short, complex, different or similar in content to the body of the question
8. Observe the use of "hedging" words – *probably, may, most likely,* etc.
9. Make sure that your answer is put next to the same number as the question
10. Do not second-guess unless you have good reason to believe the second answer is definitely more correct
11. Cross out original answer if you decide another answer is more accurate; do not erase until you are ready to hand your paper in
12. Answer all questions; guess unless instructed otherwise
13. Leave time for review

b. Essay questions
1. Read each question carefully
2. Determine exactly what is wanted. Underline key words or phrases.
3. Decide on outline or paragraph answer
4. Include many different points and elements unless asked to develop any one or two points or elements
5. Show impartiality by giving pros and cons unless directed to select one side only
6. Make and write down any assumptions you find necessary to answer the questions
7. Watch your English, grammar, punctuation and choice of words
8. Time your answers; don't crowd material

8) Answering the essay question

Most essay questions can be answered by framing the specific response around several key words or ideas. Here are a few such key words or ideas:

M's: manpower, materials, methods, money, management
P's: purpose, program, policy, plan, procedure, practice, problems, pitfalls, personnel, public relations

a. Six basic steps in handling problems:
1. Preliminary plan and background development
2. Collect information, data and facts
3. Analyze and interpret information, data and facts
4. Analyze and develop solutions as well as make recommendations
5. Prepare report and sell recommendations
6. Install recommendations and follow up effectiveness

b. Pitfalls to avoid
1. *Taking things for granted* – A statement of the situation does not necessarily imply that each of the elements is necessarily true; for example, a complaint may be invalid and biased so that all that can be taken for granted is that a complaint has been registered

2. *Considering only one side of a situation* – Wherever possible, indicate several alternatives and then point out the reasons you selected the best one
3. *Failing to indicate follow up* – Whenever your answer indicates action on your part, make certain that you will take proper follow-up action to see how successful your recommendations, procedures or actions turn out to be
4. *Taking too long in answering any single question* – Remember to time your answers properly

## IX. AFTER THE TEST

Scoring procedures differ in detail among civil service jurisdictions although the general principles are the same. Whether the papers are hand-scored or graded by machine we have described, they are nearly always graded by number. That is, the person who marks the paper knows only the number – never the name – of the applicant. Not until all the papers have been graded will they be matched with names. If other tests, such as training and experience or oral interview ratings have been given, scores will be combined. Different parts of the examination usually have different weights. For example, the written test might count 60 percent of the final grade, and a rating of training and experience 40 percent. In many jurisdictions, veterans will have a certain number of points added to their grades.

After the final grade has been determined, the names are placed in grade order and an eligible list is established. There are various methods for resolving ties between those who get the same final grade – probably the most common is to place first the name of the person whose application was received first. Job offers are made from the eligible list in the order the names appear on it. You will be notified of your grade and your rank as soon as all these computations have been made. This will be done as rapidly as possible.

People who are found to meet the requirements in the announcement are called "eligibles." Their names are put on a list of eligible candidates. An eligible's chances of getting a job depend on how high he stands on this list and how fast agencies are filling jobs from the list.

When a job is to be filled from a list of eligibles, the agency asks for the names of people on the list of eligibles for that job. When the civil service commission receives this request, it sends to the agency the names of the three people highest on this list. Or, if the job to be filled has specialized requirements, the office sends the agency the names of the top three persons who meet these requirements from the general list.

The appointing officer makes a choice from among the three people whose names were sent to him. If the selected person accepts the appointment, the names of the others are put back on the list to be considered for future openings.

That is the rule in hiring from all kinds of eligible lists, whether they are for typist, carpenter, chemist, or something else. For every vacancy, the appointing officer has his choice of any one of the top three eligibles on the list. This explains why the person whose name is on top of the list sometimes does not get an appointment when some of the persons lower on the list do. If the appointing officer chooses the second or third eligible, the No. 1 eligible does not get a job at once, but stays on the list until he is appointed or the list is terminated.

# X. HOW TO PASS THE INTERVIEW TEST

The examination for which you applied requires an oral interview test. You have already taken the written test and you are now being called for the interview test – the final part of the formal examination.

You may think that it is not possible to prepare for an interview test and that there are no procedures to follow during an interview. Our purpose is to point out some things you can do in advance that will help you and some good rules to follow and pitfalls to avoid while you are being interviewed.

*What is an interview supposed to test?*

The written examination is designed to test the technical knowledge and competence of the candidate; the oral is designed to evaluate intangible qualities, not readily measured otherwise, and to establish a list showing the relative fitness of each candidate – as measured against his competitors – for the position sought. Scoring is not on the basis of "right" and "wrong," but on a sliding scale of values ranging from "not passable" to "outstanding." As a matter of fact, it is possible to achieve a relatively low score without a single "incorrect" answer because of evident weakness in the qualities being measured.

Occasionally, an examination may consist entirely of an oral test – either an individual or a group oral. In such cases, information is sought concerning the technical knowledges and abilities of the candidate, since there has been no written examination for this purpose. More commonly, however, an oral test is used to supplement a written examination.

*Who conducts interviews?*

The composition of oral boards varies among different jurisdictions. In nearly all, a representative of the personnel department serves as chairman. One of the members of the board may be a representative of the department in which the candidate would work. In some cases, "outside experts" are used, and, frequently, a businessman or some other representative of the general public is asked to serve. Labor and management or other special groups may be represented. The aim is to secure the services of experts in the appropriate field.

However the board is composed, it is a good idea (and not at all improper or unethical) to ascertain in advance of the interview who the members are and what groups they represent. When you are introduced to them, you will have some idea of their backgrounds and interests, and at least you will not stutter and stammer over their names.

*What should be done before the interview?*

While knowledge about the board members is useful and takes some of the surprise element out of the interview, there is other preparation which is more substantive. It *is* possible to prepare for an oral interview – in several ways:

**1) Keep a copy of your application and review it carefully before the interview**

This may be the only document before the oral board, and the starting point of the interview. Know what education and experience you have listed there, and the sequence and dates of all of it. Sometimes the board will ask you to review the highlights of your experience for them; you should not have to hem and haw doing it.

**2) Study the class specification and the examination announcement**

Usually, the oral board has one or both of these to guide them. The qualities, characteristics or knowledges required by the position sought are stated in these documents. They offer valuable clues as to the nature of the oral interview. For example, if the job involves supervisory responsibilities, the announcement will usually indicate that knowledge of modern supervisory methods and the qualifications of the candidate as a supervisor will be tested. If so, you can expect such questions, frequently in the form of a hypothetical situation which you are expected to solve. NEVER go into an oral without knowledge of the duties and responsibilities of the job you seek.

### 3) Think through each qualification required

Try to visualize the kind of questions you would ask if you were a board member. How well could you answer them? Try especially to appraise your own knowledge and background in each area, *measured against the job sought*, and identify any areas in which you are weak. Be critical and realistic – do not flatter yourself.

### 4) Do some general reading in areas in which you feel you may be weak

For example, if the job involves supervision and your past experience has NOT, some general reading in supervisory methods and practices, particularly in the field of human relations, might be useful. Do NOT study agency procedures or detailed manuals. The oral board will be testing your understanding and capacity, not your memory.

### 5) Get a good night's sleep and watch your general health and mental attitude

You will want a clear head at the interview. Take care of a cold or any other minor ailment, and of course, no hangovers.

*What should be done on the day of the interview?*

Now comes the day of the interview itself. Give yourself plenty of time to get there. Plan to arrive somewhat ahead of the scheduled time, particularly if your appointment is in the fore part of the day. If a previous candidate fails to appear, the board might be ready for you a bit early. By early afternoon an oral board is almost invariably behind schedule if there are many candidates, and you may have to wait. Take along a book or magazine to read, or your application to review, but leave any extraneous material in the waiting room when you go in for your interview. In any event, relax and compose yourself.

The matter of dress is important. The board is forming impressions about you – from your experience, your manners, your attitude, and your appearance. Give your personal appearance careful attention. Dress your best, but not your flashiest. Choose conservative, appropriate clothing, and be sure it is immaculate. This is a business interview, and your appearance should indicate that you regard it as such. Besides, being well groomed and properly dressed will help boost your confidence.

Sooner or later, someone will call your name and escort you into the interview room. *This is it.* From here on you are on your own. It is too late for any more preparation. But remember, you asked for this opportunity to prove your fitness, and you are here because your request was granted.

*What happens when you go in?*

The usual sequence of events will be as follows: The clerk (who is often the board stenographer) will introduce you to the chairman of the oral board, who will introduce you to the other members of the board. Acknowledge the introductions before you sit down. Do not be surprised if you find a microphone facing you or a stenotypist sitting by. Oral interviews are usually recorded in the event of an appeal or other review.

Usually the chairman of the board will open the interview by reviewing the highlights of your education and work experience from your application – primarily for the benefit of the other members of the board, as well as to get the material into the record. Do not interrupt or comment unless there is an error or significant misinterpretation; if that is the case, do not hesitate. But do not quibble about insignificant matters. Also, he will usually ask you some question about your education, experience or your present job – partly to get you to start talking and to establish the interviewing "rapport." He may start the actual questioning, or turn it over to one of the other members. Frequently, each member undertakes the questioning on a particular area, one in which he is perhaps most competent, so you can expect each member to participate in the examination. Because time is limited, you may also expect some rather abrupt switches in the direction the questioning takes, so do not be upset by it. Normally, a board member will not pursue a single line of questioning unless he discovers a particular strength or weakness.

After each member has participated, the chairman will usually ask whether any member has any further questions, then will ask you if you have anything you wish to add. Unless you are expecting this question, it may floor you. Worse, it may start you off on an extended, extemporaneous speech. The board is not usually seeking more information. The question is principally to offer you a last opportunity to present further qualifications or to indicate that you have nothing to add. So, if you feel that a significant qualification or characteristic has been overlooked, it is proper to point it out in a sentence or so. Do not compliment the board on the thoroughness of their examination – they have been sketchy, and you know it. If you wish, merely say, "No thank you, I have nothing further to add." This is a point where you can "talk yourself out" of a good impression or fail to present an important bit of information. Remember, *you close the interview yourself.*

The chairman will then say, "That is all, Mr. _____, thank you." Do not be startled; the interview is over, and quicker than you think. Thank him, gather your belongings and take your leave. Save your sigh of relief for the other side of the door.


*How to put your best foot forward*
Throughout this entire process, you may feel that the board individually and collectively is trying to pierce your defenses, seek out your hidden weaknesses and embarrass and confuse you. Actually, this is not true. They are obliged to make an appraisal of your qualifications for the job you are seeking, and they want to see you in your best light. Remember, they must interview all candidates and a non-cooperative candidate may become a failure in spite of their best efforts to bring out his qualifications. Here are 15 suggestions that will help you:

**1) Be natural – Keep your attitude confident, not cocky**
If you are not confident that you can do the job, do not expect the board to be. Do not apologize for your weaknesses, try to bring out your strong points. The board is interested in a positive, not negative, presentation. Cockiness will antagonize any board member and make him wonder if you are covering up a weakness by a false show of strength.

**2) Get comfortable, but don't lounge or sprawl**
Sit erectly but not stiffly. A careless posture may lead the board to conclude that you are careless in other things, or at least that you are not impressed by the importance of the occasion. Either conclusion is natural, even if incorrect. Do not fuss with your clothing, a pencil or an ashtray. Your hands may occasionally be useful to emphasize a point; do not let them become a point of distraction.

**3) Do not wisecrack or make small talk**
This is a serious situation, and your attitude should show that you consider it as such. Further, the time of the board is limited – they do not want to waste it, and neither should you.

### 4) Do not exaggerate your experience or abilities

In the first place, from information in the application or other interviews and sources, the board may know more about you than you think. Secondly, you probably will not get away with it. An experienced board is rather adept at spotting such a situation, so do not take the chance.

### 5) If you know a board member, do not make a point of it, yet do not hide it

Certainly you are not fooling him, and probably not the other members of the board. Do not try to take advantage of your acquaintanceship – it will probably do you little good.

### 6) Do not dominate the interview

Let the board do that. They will give you the clues – do not assume that you have to do all the talking. Realize that the board has a number of questions to ask you, and do not try to take up all the interview time by showing off your extensive knowledge of the answer to the first one.

### 7) Be attentive

You only have 20 minutes or so, and you should keep your attention at its sharpest throughout. When a member is addressing a problem or question to you, give him your undivided attention. Address your reply principally to him, but do not exclude the other board members.

### 8) Do not interrupt

A board member may be stating a problem for you to analyze. He will ask you a question when the time comes. Let him state the problem, and wait for the question.

### 9) Make sure you understand the question

Do not try to answer until you are sure what the question is. If it is not clear, restate it in your own words or ask the board member to clarify it for you. However, do not haggle about minor elements.

### 10) Reply promptly but not hastily

A common entry on oral board rating sheets is "candidate responded readily," or "candidate hesitated in replies." Respond as promptly and quickly as you can, but do not jump to a hasty, ill-considered answer.

### 11) Do not be peremptory in your answers

A brief answer is proper – but do not fire your answer back. That is a losing game from your point of view. The board member can probably ask questions much faster than you can answer them.

### 12) Do not try to create the answer you think the board member wants

He is interested in what kind of mind you have and how it works – not in playing games. Furthermore, he can usually spot this practice and will actually grade you down on it.

### 13) Do not switch sides in your reply merely to agree with a board member

Frequently, a member will take a contrary position merely to draw you out and to see if you are willing and able to defend your point of view. Do not start a debate, yet do not surrender a good position. If a position is worth taking, it is worth defending.

**14) Do not be afraid to admit an error in judgment if you are shown to be wrong**

The board knows that you are forced to reply without any opportunity for careful consideration. Your answer may be demonstrably wrong. If so, admit it and get on with the interview.

**15) Do not dwell at length on your present job**

The opening question may relate to your present assignment. Answer the question but do not go into an extended discussion. You are being examined for a *new* job, not your present one. As a matter of fact, try to phrase ALL your answers in terms of the job for which you are being examined.

*Basis of Rating*

Probably you will forget most of these "do's" and "don'ts" when you walk into the oral interview room. Even remembering them all will not ensure you a passing grade. Perhaps you did not have the qualifications in the first place. But remembering them will help you to put your best foot forward, without treading on the toes of the board members.

Rumor and popular opinion to the contrary notwithstanding, an oral board wants you to make the best appearance possible. They know you are under pressure – but they also want to see how you respond to it as a guide to what your reaction would be under the pressures of the job you seek. They will be influenced by the degree of poise you display, the personal traits you show and the manner in which you respond.

ABOUT THIS BOOK

This book contains tests divided into Examination Sections. Go through each test, answering every question in the margin. We have also attached a sample answer sheet at the back of the book that can be removed and used. At the end of each test look at the answer key and check your answers. On the ones you got wrong, look at the right answer choice and learn. Do not fill in the answers first. Do not memorize the questions and answers, but understand the answer and principles involved. On your test, the questions will likely be different from the samples. Questions are changed and new ones added. If you understand these past questions you should have success with any changes that arise. Tests may consist of several types of questions. We have additional books on each subject should more study be advisable or necessary for you. Finally, the more you study, the better prepared you will be. This book is intended to be the last thing you study before you walk into the examination room. Prior study of relevant texts is also recommended. NLC publishes some of these in our Fundamental Series. Knowledge and good sense are important factors in passing your exam. Good luck also helps. So now study this Passbook, absorb the material contained within and take that knowledge into the examination. Then do your best to pass that exam.

# EXAMINATION SECTION

# EXAMINATION SECTION

# TEST 1

DIRECTIONS: Each question or incomplete statement is followed by several suggested answers or completions. Select the one that BEST answers the question or completes the statement. *PRINT THE LETTER OF THE CORRECT ANSWER IN THE SPACE AT THE RIGHT.*

1. An unusually high vacuum reading in a fuel oil suction line may indicate that the
    A. level in the fuel oil tank is low
    B. oil preheater is leaking
    C. oil strainer is dirty
    D. oil is too hot

2. The MAIN reason for modulating the flame in a steam heating boiler that has an automatic rotary cup oil burner is to
    A. reduce the number of start and stop operations
    B. guarantee a high-fire start
    C. vary the cut-out pressure
    D. vary the cut-in pressure

3. The device on a rotary cup oil burner which senses primary air failure is the
    A. draft sensing device
    B. aquastat
    C. draft alarm
    D. vaporstat

4. A 10,000-gallon pressurized house tank contains 8,030 gallons of water, and the pressure gauge reads 60 psi. In the event of a power failure, the number of gallons of water which can be drawn out of the tank before the pressure reading drops to 50 psi is MOST NEARLY
    A. 300   B. 2,000   C. 6,000   D. 8,000

5. The heat balancer in a Dunham steam heating system
    A. measures indoor temperatures
    B. controls the firing rate of two or more boilers
    C. measures outdoor temperatures
    D. reacts to the rate of heat output

6. In a sub-atmospheric steam heating system, the steam temperature corresponding to a vacuum of 15 inches of mercury is MOST NEARLY _____ °F.
    A. 180   B. 200   C. 212   D. 218

7. When the fuel supply to a rotary cup oil burner is cut off, the burner motor switch should open within _____ seconds.
    A. 2   B. 4 to 8   C. 12 to 18   D. 30 to 40

8. The proper method of laying up a steam boiler, for a period of less than one month, is to
    A. drain all the water and let the boiler dry out
    B. fill it with treated water to the top of the tubes
    C. fill it with treated water to the stop valve
    D. fill it with treated water to the level of the upper try cock

9. In the winter time, heating complaints by tenants should be investigated
    A. only if there are several complaints from one building
    B. only if the outside temperature is below 40°F
    C. immediately
    D. by the assistant superintendent

10. Compared to the input of an electric ignition transformer associated with #6 oil burners, the output is _____ voltage, _____ current.
    A. higher; higher
    B. higher; lower
    C. lower; higher
    D. lower; lower

11. A pressure regulator valve in a compressed air line should be
    A. preceded by a water and oil separator
    B. preceded by a solenoid valve
    C. followed by a water and oil separator
    D. followed by a solenoid valve

12. A preventive maintenance program in a boiler room should provide for the routine periodic replacement of
    A. badly leaking boiler tubes
    B. electric motors
    C. safety valve springs
    D. programmer electronic tubes

13. Steam-heated hot water tank coils can be tested for leaks by
    A. chemically testing the domestic hot water leaving the tank
    B. chemically testing the condensate leaving the coil
    C. pressure testing the domestic water in the tank
    D. pressure testing the condensate return

14. The chemical which is added to boiler water to reduce its oxygen content is sodium
    A. carbonate
    B. chloride
    C. alginate
    D. sulphite

15. Wear in the sleeve bearings of an electric motor is MOST likely to result in a change in the
    A. pole spacing
    B. armature balance
    C. air gap
    D. line frequency

16. *Found reading* and *left reading* are terms associated with
    A. petrometers
    B. electric meters
    C. gas meters
    D. water meters

17. The FIRST priority in snow removal in a housing project is to remove snow from the
    A. building entrance steps and entrance landings
    B. perimeter sidewalks
    C. access to fuel oil fill lines and fire hydrants
    D. interior sidewalks leading from buildings to perimeter sidewalks

18. On Memorial Day, the National Flag should be flown at
    A. full staff all day
    B. half staff in the morning and full staff from noon to sunset
    C. half staff all day
    D. full staff in the morning and at half staff from noon to sunset

19. The common name for a tree called Quercus Alba is
    A. pine
    B. maple
    C. oak
    D. cedar

20. A tree which is considered to be suitable for street curb planting should
    A. grow rapidly
    B. have colorful foliage
    C. be an evergreen
    D. be straight and symmetrical

21. A roofing bond is
    A. the material used to cement the roofing layers to each other
    B. a guarantee by the manufacturer of the roofing material
    C. a guarantee by the contractor who installed the roof
    D. a vapor barrier

22. Window shade cloth has a calculated service life of _____ years.
    A. 2    B. 4    C. 6    D. 8

23. A resin-base floor finish USUALLY
    A. gives the highest luster of all floor finishes
    B. cannot be used on asphalt tile
    C. must be applied in heavy coats
    D. provides an anti-slip surface

24. The cause of paint blisters on wood is USUALLY
    A. moisture under the paint coat
    B. too thick a coat of paint
    C. too much oil in the paint
    D. plaster pores not sealed properly

25. When waxing asphalt tile floors, the wax should be applied in several thin coats because
    A. one thick coat takes longer to apply
    B. it will dry faster and harder
    C. it is a more economical method
    D. the pores of the tile will be able to absorb the wax more readily

26. A supplier quotes a list price of $14.00 for a replacement part less discounts of 25, 10 and 5 percent. The cost of the item is MOST NEARLY
    A. $5.50   B. $6.00   C. $8.50   D. $9.00

27. Assuming that it requires 6 man-days to replace a sidewalk 4 feet wide x 120 feet long, then a similar sidewalk 8 feet wide x 78 feet long would require MOST NEARLY _____ man-days.
    A. 6   B. 8   C. 10   D. 14

28. The initials S.S., as used in connection with window glass, means
    A. single strength
    B. single silicon
    C. sharp section
    D. striated surface

29. If a screwed galvanized iron fitting is used in a copper or brass line, the MOST probable result would be that the
    A. galvanized iron fitting will rust quickly
    B. brass line will have to be replaced
    C. galvanized fitting will outlast the brass line
    D. brass line will corrode

30. A plumbing sketch is drawn to a scale of 1/8" = 1 foot. A horizontal water line measuring 6 3/4" on the sketch would be equivalent to _____ feet of water pipe.
    A. 27   B. 41   C. 54   D. 64

31. The tool that holds the die when threading a 2" pipe is called a
    A. yoke
    B. punch
    C. vise
    D. stock

32. Of the following, the BEST fastener to use in a hollow wall is the _____ bolt.
    A. expansion
    B. carriage
    C. machine nut and
    D. toggle

33. A 5 hp, 3 phase, 208-volt squirrel cage motor is USUALLY started by means of a(n)
    A. compensator
    B. across the line starter
    C. reduced voltage starter
    D. 3 point starting box

34. When using a voltmeter in testing an electric circuit, the voltmeter should be connected
    A. across the circuit
    B. in series with the circuit
    C. in parallel or series with the circuit
    D. in series with the active element

35. The coloring material in an exterior wall paint is called the
    A. solvent
    B. lacquer
    C. vehicle
    D. pigment

## KEY (CORRECT ANSWERS)

| | | | |
|---|---|---|---|
| 1. C | 11. A | 21. B | 31. D |
| 2. A | 12. D | 22. C | 32. D |
| 3. D | 13. B | 23. D | 33. B |
| 4. A | 14. D | 24. A | 34. A |
| 5. D | 15. C | 25. B | 35. D |
| 6. A | 16. B | 26. D | |
| 7. B | 17. C | 27. B | |
| 8. C | 18. B | 28. A | |
| 9. C | 19. C | 29. A | |
| 10. B | 20. D | 30. C | |

# TEST 2

DIRECTIONS: Each question or incomplete statement is followed by several suggested answers or completions. Select the one that BEST answers the question or completes the statement. *PRINT THE LETTER OF THE CORRECT ANSWER IN THE SPACE AT THE RIGHT.*

1. The refrigerant MOST often used in household refrigerators is
   A. argon
   B. lithium bromide
   C. ammonia
   D. freon-12

   1._____

2. When tie or identical low bids are submitted for a competitive contract under $1,000 by two bidders, the successful bidder may be selected by
   A. requesting a new bid from a third party
   B. tossing a coin
   C. drawing lots
   D. requesting new bids from all the bidders and selecting the lowest bid

   2._____

3. The one of the following which is LEAST important in developing a budget for the next fiscal year for project maintenance is the
   A. adequacy of the current year's budget
   B. changes in workload that can be anticipated
   C. budget restrictions indicated in a memorandum covering budget preparations
   D. staff reassignments which are expected during the next fiscal year

   3._____

4. The LEAST likely subject to be discussed at a planning meeting with assistant superintendents and foremen is the
   A. allocation of responsibility for the phases of administration
   B. provision for coordination and follow-up
   C. setting goals for each supervisor's section
   D. assignment of tasks to individual workers

   4._____

5. From the standpoint of equal opportunity, the MOST critical item that a superintendent should focus on is
   A. assigning only minority workers to supervisory positions
   B. helping minority employees to upgrade their knowledge so they may qualify for higher positions
   C. placing minority workers in job categories above their present level of ability so that they can "sink" or "swim"
   D. disregarding merit system principles

   5._____

6. After careful deliberation, you have decided that one of your workers should be disciplined. It is MOST important that the
   A. discipline be severe for best results
   B. discipline be delayed as long as possible
   C. worker understands why he is being disciplined
   D. other workers be consulted before the discipline is administered

   6._____

7. Of the following, the MOST important qualities of an employee chosen for a supervisory position are
    A. education and intelligence
    B. interest in the objectives and activities of the agency
    C. skill in performing the type of work to be supervised
    D. knowledge of the work and leadership ability

8. A tenant complains to you that he was wet by the spray from a garden hose handled carelessly by one of your workers and that he can identify the worker. The BEST course of action is for you to
    A. express regret and assure the tenant that you will caution the worker
    B. try to convince the tenant that he did not get too wet
    C. assure the tenant that charges will be preferred against the worker
    D. arrange a meeting between tenant and worker and make the worker apologize

9. In preparing a report to his supervisor, a superintendent should
    A. include irrelevant matters to show a greater grasp of the problem
    B. not allow anyone to read and criticize the draft of the report for fear that he will seem incompetent
    C. prepare an outline before writing the draft of the report
    D. always question whether or not the report is necessary

10. A superintendent who is preparing a report on a study which was requested by his supervisor should make the FIRST section of the report a discussion of the
    A. situation which exists currently
    B. method of instituting the recommendations
    C. objections to the report
    D. additional equipment needed to carry out the recommendations

11. A superintendent should read the work orders for the maintenance men each morning so that
    A. every work order is completed the day it is received
    B. all work orders are handled in chronological order regardless of the kind of work involved
    C. the work which the maintenance men do not like to do is not postponed continually
    D. the maintenance men know that you are checking up on them every minute of the day

12. MOST tenants in a housing project will
    A. separate in their minds the actions of a superintendent and the policies of the housing authority
    B. consider what the superintendent does as the policy of the housing authority
    C. realize that superintendents will follow policies that are undesirable to the housing authority
    D. make allowances for the policies a superintendent follows

13. Mortar joints in old brickwork are BEST repaired by
    A. setting
    B. framing
    C. taping
    D. pointing

14. An equipment rental allowance includes the rental charge plus 9%. If a piece of equipment is rented for 11 days at $36 per day, the total equipment allowance is MOST NEARLY
    A. $360   B. $390   C. $420   D. $450

15. The extinguishing agent in a soda-acid fire extinguisher is
    A. water
    B. hydrochloric acid
    C. sodium bicarbonate
    D. carbon dioxide

16. A building heated by an oil-fired boiler used 3,500 gallons of oil during a period of 2100 degree days. The number of gallons of oil that probably would be burned by the same building over a period of 1800 degree days is
    A. 2700   B. 3000   C. 3400   D. 3700

17. Of the following, the BEST chemical to use to melt ice on pavements is
    A. carbon tetrachloride
    B. calcium chloride
    C. potassium hydroxide
    D. sodium fluoride

18. The MAIN purpose of periodic inspection and tests of electrical equipment is to
    A. encourage workers to take better care of the equipment
    B. familiarize the workers with the equipment
    C. keep the workers busy during otherwise slack periods
    D. discover minor faults before they develop into major faults

19. The greatest benefit of job evaluation is in
    A. placing the blame for inefficiency
    B. testing the intelligence of custodial workers
    C. eliminating duplication of activities
    D. determining efficiency ratings

20. The current rating of the fuse to use in a lighting circuit is determined by the
    A. connected load
    B. line voltage
    C. capacity of the wiring
    D. rating of the switch

21. Portable fire extinguishers which are suitable for Class C fires should be identified by the letter C inside a
    A. triangle
    B. circle
    C. square
    D. five-point star

22. In the piping system for domestic gas supply,
    A. risers must have a drip leg and cap at the bottom
    B. gasketed unions are used to join pipes
    C. couplings with running threads are used to join pipes
    D. composition disc globe valves are used to throttle the gas

23. A cast iron soil pipe-bend having an angle of 45 degrees is COMMONLY called a _____ bend.
    A. 1/16   B. 1/8   C. 1/4   D. return

24. Of the following, the LEAST likely cause of faulty atomization of fuel oil in a rotary cup oil burner is
    A. too low an oil temperature
    B. too low an oil pressure
    C. insufficient secondary air
    D. insufficient primary air

25. In order to minimize the labor involved in replacing an electric motor, which is directly connected to a centrifugal house pump, the specification for the new motor should include the
    A. shaft size
    B. NEMA frame size
    C. end bell size
    D. NEMA design letter

26. The supervisor of a large group of maintenance workers will most likely find that the GREATEST number of them will be motivated by
    A. letting them plan and control their own work
    B. giving them more responsibility
    C. supervising them very closely
    D. considering each of them individually and treating them accordingly

27. An example of a non-flammable liquid is
    A. floor sealer
    B. kerosene
    C. carbon tetrachloride
    D. benzene

28. Which of the following malfunctions is MOST hazardous to life?  28._____
    A. Short circuit in an outlet box
    B. Gas leak from a stove connection
    C. Water leak behind a kitchen sink
    D. Steam leak from a stop valve

29. A supervisor observes that there is a constant backlog of work tickets, which results in a long delay between the time when a complaint is reported by a tenant and when the work is completed.  29._____
    In handling this situation, the supervisor should
    A. ignore the situation if he is certain he can avoid being blamed for it
    B. ignore the situation because it is really the responsibility of the superintendent
    C. explain the situation to the superintendent and recommend waiting until the situation gets so bad that the central office will realize that more permanent maintenance men are needed
    D. explain the situation to the superintendent and recommend that he request the loan of several maintenance men from the central office for sufficient time to reduce the backlog to normal

30. A supervisor assigns a maintenance man to do an emergency job and gives him the authority to obtain the help and equipment he needs to complete the job.  30._____
    Under these circumstances, FINAL responsibility for the job
    A. belongs to the maintenance man
    B. remains with the supervisor
    C. cannot be determined
    D. is shared between the maintenance man and the supervisor

## KEY (CORRECT ANSWERS)

| | | |
|---|---|---|
| 1. D | 11. C | 21. B |
| 2. C | 12. B | 22. A |
| 3. D | 13. D | 23. B |
| 4. D | 14. C | 24. C |
| 5. B | 15. A | 25. B |
| 6. C | 16. B | 26. D |
| 7. D | 17. B | 27. C |
| 8. A | 18. D | 28. B |
| 9. C | 19. C | 29. D |
| 10. A | 20. C | 30. B |

# EXAMINATION SECTION
# TEST 1

DIRECTIONS: Each question or incomplete statement is followed by several suggested answers or completions. Select the one that BEST answers the question or completes the statement. *PRINT THE LETTER OF THE CORRECT ANSWER IN THE SPACE AT THE RIGHT.*

1. An instrument that is USUALLY mounted on a boiler control panel and which is read in inches of water is known as a(n) _____ gauge.  1.____

   A. pressure  B. draft
   C. stack temperature  D. Orsat indicator

2. The type of pump which should be used to supply fuel oil to a low-pressure boiler is the _____ pump.  2.____

   A. centrifugal  B. diaphragm  C. rotary gear  D. reciprocating

3. A thermostatic radiator trap which is working satisfactorily will  3.____

   A. *open* to pass the steam  B. *open* to pass the condensate
   C. *close* to retain the cool air  D. *close* to retain the condensate

4. Readings of stack temperature and percentage of carbon dioxide are useful in the boiler room in determining changes in the boiler's _____ efficiency.  4.____

   A. mechanical  B. volumetric  C. overall  D. combustion

5. In the start-up cycle of a boiler which is equipped with all of the following devices, the device that should be energized BEFORE all the others is the  5.____

   A. magnetic oil valve  B. ignition transformer
   C. gas solenoid valve  D. fresh air louvre motor

6. The one of the following valves which is electrically operated is the _____ valve.  6.____

   A. pressure relief  B. magnetic oil
   C. check  D. thermostatic control

7. In an installation where there is only one fuel-oil pump set, a duplex strainer is PREFERABLY used because  7.____

   A. one side of the strainer can be cleaned without interrupting the flow of oil
   B. one side of the strainer will screen out much finer particles than the other side
   C. the flow of oil can be directed through both sides at the same time, thereby increasing the velocity of the oil
   D. cleaning of a duplex strainer is not required during the heating season

8. A higher-than-normal vacuum reading on a gauge which is attached to the suction side of a fuel-oil pump generally indicates that there is  8.____

   A. no oil in the tank
   B. a clogged strainer in the suction line
   C. a broken fitting in the suction line
   D. worn packing on the pump

9. The one of the following which is NOT a possible point of entry of water leaking into the fuel-oil storage tank is the

    A. fuel fill pipe can
    B. sounding well plug
    C. steam coil in a fuel-oil heater
    D. fire box side of the furnace wall

10. When an air vaporstat which is connected to an automatic rotary cup oil burner senses the loss of primary air pressure in the fan housing, it *de-energizes* the

    A. burner motor-starter coil
    B. magnetic-oil valve
    C. secondary air-damper control
    D. modutrol motor

11. A steam boiler which is externally fired and in which the hot gases pass through the tubes is commonly known as a _____ boiler.

    A. Scotch           B. locomotive
    C. horizontal return tubular    D. vertical tubular

12. The modulating pressuretrol on an automatic rotary cup oil-fired boiler controls the

    A. modutrol motor circuit      B. magnetic oil valve
    C. burner motor starter        D. electric heater

13. The reason for *blowing down* a boiler is to

    A. *lower* the boiler water level below the boiler tubes
    B. *reduce* the concentration of dissolved solids in the boiler water
    C. *reduce* the concentration of dissolved oxygen in the boiler water
    D. *eliminate* the need for treating the boiler water chemically

14. The one of the following boiler pressure-actuated devices which should be adjusted to operate at the highest pre-sure setting is the

    A. pop-safety valve
    B. manual-reset pressuretrol
    C. modulating pressuretrol
    D. limit pressuretrol

15. The BEST procedure for testing the operation of a low-water cutout is to *lower* the _____ until the burner shuts off.

    A. boiler water level *rapidly*
    B. boiler water level *slowly*
    C. water level in the water column *rapidly*
    D. water level in the water column *slowly*

16. If the water disappears from the gauge glass on a low-pressure oil-fired boiler, the FIRST action the boiler operator should take is to

    A. shut off the water
    B. add water to the boiler until the glass fills up to the correct level
    C. open the bottom blow-down valve
    D. blow down the water column

17. On a certain day, the lowest outside temperature was 20° F and the highest was 40° F. The number of degree days for this day is

    A. 25    B. 30    C. 35    D. 45

18. A vacuum return line pump should NOT be operated with the electrical control set for

    A. continuous operation
    B. float and vacuum control
    C. float control only
    D. vacuum control only

19. The PREFERRED location for a Dunham Selector is on the _____ exposure of the building.

    A. north    B. east    C. south    D. west

20. Maintaining a Dunham Heat Balancer in good working order requires *annual* cleaning of its

    A. radiator fins
    B. relay contacts
    C. solenoid valve
    D. fulcrum

21. A chemical useful in reducing the concentration of oxygen in boiler water is

    A. tannin
    B. amines
    C. sodium sulphite
    D. sodium carbonate

22. Smoke alarms which must be installed on oil-fired boilers should create a loud signal and a red flashing light upon the emission of an air contaminant whose density, when compared to the standard smoke chart, appears darker than Number _____ on the chart.

    A. 1    B. 2    C. 3    D. 4

23. Samples for the testing of boiler water should be taken from the

    A. bottom blow-off
    B. condensate tank
    C. water column
    D. condensate-return line

24. In a building which is heated by an oil-fired boiler, 2,100 gallons of fuel oil were burned in a period in which the degree days reached a total of 1,400.
    If all other conditions remained constant, the number of gallons of fuel oil that would be burned in this building during a period in which the degree days reached a total of 3,600 is

    A. 2,400    B. 2,900    C. 4,800    D. 5,400

25. Of the following fuels, the one with the HIGHEST viscosity is

    A. kerosene    B. natural gas    C. #6 oil    D. #2 oil

## KEY (CORRECT ANSWERS)

| | | | |
|---|---|---|---|
| 1. | B | 11. | C |
| 2. | C | 12. | A |
| 3. | B | 13. | B |
| 4. | D | 14. | A |
| 5. | D | 15. | B |
| 6. | B | 16. | A |
| 7. | A | 17. | C |
| 8. | B | 18. | D |
| 9. | D | 19. | A |
| 10. | B | 20. | A |

21. C
22. A
23. C
24. D
25. C

# TEST 2

DIRECTIONS: Each question or incomplete statement is followed by several suggested answers or completions. Select the one that BEST answers the question or completes the statement. *PRINT THE LETTER OF THE CORRECT ANSWER IN THE SPACE AT THE RIGHT.*

1. The device which **protects** the boiler from damage due to low water is the

   A. fusible plug          B. fusible link
   C. vaporstat             D. aquastat

2. In a low-pressure fire-tube boiler, the oil burner should be shut off BEFORE

   A. operating the soot blower
   B. taking a flue gas sample
   C. blowing down the boiler
   D. blowing down the water column

3. A domestic hot water circulating pump is started and stopped automatically by means of a(n) _____ in the line.

   A. pressuretrol; supply       B. pressuretrol; return
   C. aquastat; supply           D. aquastat; return

4. On a steam-heated domestic hot water generator, the device which acts to *prevent* damage to the coils due to a high internal pressure differential between the coil and the tank is the

   A. pressure relief valve      B. vacuum breaker
   C. air vent valve             D. steam trap

5. In the city, the rules and regulations concerning the cleaning of a water tank which is part of a building's domestic water supply are specified by the

   A. fire department
   B. department of housing and buildings
   C. city sanitary code
   D. board of water supply

6. A housing fireman, making a preliminary inspection of a fuel oil delivery truck, discovers that the level of the oil in one compartment is far below the marker.
   In this case, he SHOULD

   A. reject the shipment and order that it be returned to the terminal
   B. measure the level of the oil in the low compartment by *sticking* and report his findings to the superintendent before unloading
   C. read the liquidometer gauge before allowing the truck to be unloaded and again after it has been unloaded and record the difference in gallons to determine the amount for which payment should be made
   D. ignore the low level if it is in only one compartment

7. Of the following fire extinguishers, the one which should be provided for use in the elevator machine room is the _____ type.

    A. carbon dioxide
    B. soda-acid
    C. foam
    D. loaded-stream

8. The wall surface which does NOT have to be washed from the bottom up to avoid streaking is a(n) _____ wall.

    A. semi-gloss painted
    B. enamel painted
    C. glazed tile
    D. unglazed tile

9. The one of the following practices which is GENERALLY recommended to prolong the useful life of a corn broom is

    A. soaking a new broom overnight before using it for the first time to remove brittleness
    B. storing the broom with the tips of the straws resting on the floor to keep the edges even
    C. keeping the straws moistened when sweeping
    D. storing the broom in a warm humid enclosure to prevent drying of the bristles

10. While a caretaker is sweeping the public corridors and stairways, he notices some crayon marks on walls and stains on the floors.
    He SHOULD

    A. stop sweeping and remove the stains immediately
    B. finish sweeping and then return to remove the stains
    C. make note of the marks and stains in his building and remove them once a month
    D. make a note of the marks and stains and report them to the superintendent so that the cause can be eliminated before the stains are removed

11. When transporting the equipment required for mopping stairhalls and corridors, a caretaker should NOT

    A. attempt to do it alone
    B. carry water in the pails because spillage may cause a tenant to slip and fall
    C. use the elevator
    D. carry the equipment in both hands when climbing stairs

12. A caretaker should apply washing solution to a portion of a painted wall and should rinse the same area before applying the solution to another area.
    In order to allow sufficient time for the solution to take effect on the soil, the area covered each time should be APPROXIMATELY _____ square feet.

    A. 20   B. 60   C. 160   D. 600

13. Asphalt tile floors should be maintained by coating them with

    A. water emulsion wax
    B. paste wax
    C. oil emulsion wax
    D. neat's-foot oil

14. The broom with which a caretaker should sweep an asphalt-paved playground is the _____ broom.

    A. hair   B. corn   C. garage   D. Scotch

15. A paper sticker should be used by a caretaker to  15.____

    A. pick up litter and fruit skins
    B. make temporary warning signs to be placed around wet floor areas
    C. indicate on the elevator panel on which floor he is working
    D. feed old newspapers into the incinerator

16. The type of floor which should be cleaned by sweeping and then mopping with an abrasive detergent is the _____ floor.  16.____

    A. painted cement          B. unpainted cement
    C. asphalt tile            D. terrazzo

17. The term *cutting the water* refers to one step in the procedure for  17.____

    A. cleaning windows        B. treating boiler water
    C. watering lawns          D. washing walls

18. Stains on ceramic tile may be removed by very carefully using a dilute solution of _____ acid.  18.____

    A. acetic                  B. oxalic
    C. sulphuric               D. hydrochloric

19. The directions on the label of a bottle of detergent call for mixing four ounces of detergent with one gallon of water to make a cleaning solution for washing floors.  19.____
    In order to obtain a LARGER amount of solution of the same strength, one quart of the detergent should be mixed with _____ gallons of water.

    A. 2          B. 4          C. 6          D. 8

20. Garden soil which has a pH reading of 6.0 is said to be  20.____

    A. neutral                 B. slightly acid
    C. slightly alkaline       D. strongly acid

21. Acid soil can be treated so that the acidity is reduced by using  21.____

    A. limestone               B. peat moss
    C. humus                   D. nitrogen

22. The one of the following procedures which is NOT recommended for growing turfgrass in shaded areas is to  22.____

    A. fertilize more frequently than normal
    B. water deeply and frequently
    C. compact the soil as much as possible
    D. prune shallow tree roots as much as possible

23. Hedges should be trimmed so that the top is _____ than the bottom with the solid leaf growth starting _____ the ground.  23.____

    A. *narrower;* about eighteen inches above
    B. *narrower;* as close as possible to
    C. *wider;* about eighteen inches above
    D. *wider;* as close as possible to

24. A checklist of outdoor tasks which should be performed in March and April should NOT include

    A. fertilizing lawn areas
    B. applying dormant spray
    C. cleaning window wells
    D. spraying broad-leaved weeds

25. Lawns should be mowed when the grass has attained a height of _____ inch(es) with the mower set at _____ inch(es).

    A. 4; 3        B. 3; 2        C. 2; 1        D. 1; 1/2

---

# KEY (CORRECT ANSWERS)

| | | | |
|---|---|---|---|
| 1. A | | 11. D | |
| 2. C | | 12. C | |
| 3. D | | 13. A | |
| 4. B | | 14. C | |
| 5. C | | 15. A | |
| 6. B | | 16. B | |
| 7. A | | 17. A | |
| 8. C | | 18. D | |
| 9. A | | 19. D | |
| 10. B | | 20. B | |

21. A
22. C
23. B
24. D
25. B

# TEST 3

DIRECTIONS: Each question or incomplete statement is followed by several suggested answers or completions. Select the one that BEST answers the question or completes the statement. *PRINT THE LETTER OF THE CORRECT ANSWER IN THE SPACE AT THE RIGHT.*

1. The number of employees required for raising the national flag in the morning and lowering it at night is:
   _____ employee(s) to raise; _____ employee(s) to lower and fold it.

   A. One; one   B. One; two   C. Two; two   D. Two; one

2. The component of fertilizers which aids in keeping grass from turning brown in the summer time is

   A. limestone   B. calcium   C. chlordane   D. nitrogen

3. The one of the following chemicals which can be used to melt ice on sidewalks is

   A. carbon tetrachloride   B. methane
   C. acetic acid   D. sodium chloride

4. A snow fence, which is used to prevent the drifting of snow over certain areas, is USUALLY made of

   A. wood slats wired together
   B. plastic-coated woven wire
   C. compacted snow
   D. two horizontal wood rails joining vertical posts

5. The area of a lawn which is 58 feet wide by 96 feet long is MOST NEARLY _____ square feet.

   A. 5000   B. 5500   C. 6000   D. 6500

6. All elevators must be inspected by the department of

   A. buildings   B. air resources
   C. health   D. labor

7. The training of personnel in the procedure for restoring stalled elevators to service and releasing passengers from stalled elevators should be given by the

   A. project superintendent
   B. chief superintendent
   C. project elevator mechanic
   D. project assistant superintendent

8. When a maintenance man is greasing a ball bearing pillow block which is equipped with shaft seals, he should pump grease through the grease fitting UNTIL

   A. a strong back pressure is felt on the gun
   B. grease starts to leak past both seals
   C. clean grease starts to leak out of the opened drain hole
   D. six strokes of the gun handle are counted

9. In buildings, safety checks of every elevator hatch door should be made each day by the

   A. caretaker  B. elevator mechanic
   C. assistant superintendent  D. maintenance man

10. The BEST way to find a Freon 12 refrigerant leak in a domestic refrigerator is by using a

    A. sulphur match  B. plumber's candle
    C. peroxide bath  D. halide torch

11. Good preventive maintenance of mechanical equipment in a housing project should result in an INCREASE in the

    A. frequency of unscheduled repairs  B. overall cost of maintenance
    C. down-time of the equipment  D. efficiency of service

12. In a building, plexiglass can be used to replace ordinary glass which is located in

    A. apartments that are more than 150 feet above curb level
    B. stairhalls
    C. front entrance doors
    D. fire-resistive opening protective assemblies

13. The BEST bit to use in an electric drill when drilling a hole in masonry is a(n)

    A. high-speed steel bit  B. auger
    C. carbide-tipped bit  D. tapered-shank tool steel bit

14. The type of fastener used to attach a butt hinge to a metal door is a

    A. round head rivet  B. flat head machine screw
    C. filister head cap screw  D. flat head wood screw

15. Burner gas cocks on kitchen stoves should be lubricated when necessary with

    A. refrigerant oil  B. graphited grease
    C. penetrating oil  D. cutting oil

16. A type of portable tool used to bend electrical conduit is called a

    A. helve  B. newel  C. spandrel  D. hickey

17. A device used to guide a handsaw to cut boards at a desired angle to form an evenly divided angle joint is called a

    A. miter box  B. backsaw  C. try square  D. protractor

18. The criteria governing preventive maintenance of vehicles require that all of the following be done at certain intervals.
    The one which must be done MOST frequently is

    A. changing the engine oil
    B. changing the engine oil filter
    C. checking the radiator coolant level
    D. rotating the tires

19. Only the plug on the electric cord of a refrigerator gets very hot when the refrigerator is operating normally. The MOST likely cause of this is that there is a(n)  19.____

    A. poor electrical connection in the plug
    B. oversized fuse in the circuit
    C. short circuit in the plug
    D. short circuit in the motor

20. Of two back-to-back plumbing fixtures are stopped up at the same time, the stoppage is MOST likely in the  20.____

    A. trap of one of the fixtures
    B. waste line in the wall
    C. vent line in the wall
    D. vacuum breaker

21. The procedure which should be followed to stop a faucet drip in a faucet which is equipped with non-renewable seats is to replace  21.____

    A. the faucet with a new one
    B. all the washers and seats with new ones
    C. all the washers with new ones and grind the seats until smooth
    D. both spindles

22. The ADVANTAGE of using a flexible coupling over using a rigid coupling on the shaft of a house pump is that the flexible coupling  22.____

    A. allows for slight misalignment of the shafts
    B. can transmit more power than a rigid coupling
    C. provides a cushioned start
    D. prevents overloading of the motor

23. The one of the following attitudes which a good supervisor should encourage among his subordinates is that they  23.____

    A. should want to do the best possible job
    B. should work only well enough to get by
    C. do not work as hard as the workers in other projects
    D. must produce more work each day than they did on the previous day

24. The supervisory function which deals with the determination of what work a supervisor wants done by his staff is known as  24.____

    A. planning           B. staffing
    C. directing          D. controlling

25. The one of the following personality traits that is UNDESIRABLE is  25.____

    A. self-confidence    B. intelligence
    C. initiative         D. indifference

## KEY (CORRECT ANSWERS)

| | | | |
|---|---|---|---|
| 1. | B | 11. | D |
| 2. | D | 12. | C |
| 3. | D | 13. | C |
| 4. | A | 14. | B |
| 5. | B | 15. | B |
| 6. | A | 16. | D |
| 7. | C | 17. | A |
| 8. | C | 18. | C |
| 9. | A | 19. | A |
| 10. | D | 20. | B |

21. C
22. A
23. A
24. A
25. D

# EXAMINATION SECTION
# TEST 1

DIRECTIONS: Each question or incomplete statement is followed by several suggested answers or completions. Select the one that BEST answers the question or completes the statement. *PRINT THE LETTER OF THE CORRECT ANSWER IN THE SPACE AT THE RIGHT.*

1. Two cleaners swept four corridors in 24 minutes. Each corridor measured 12 feet x 176 feet.
   The space swept per man per minute was MOST NEARLY _____ square feet.

   A. 50  B. 90  C. 180  D. 350

   1._____

2. The BEST time of the day to dust classroom furniture and woodwork is

   A. in the morning before the students arrive
   B. during the morning recess
   C. during the students' lunch time
   D. immediately after the students are dismissed for the day

   2._____

3. A custodian-engineer wishes to order sponges in the most economical manner. Keeping in mind that large sponges can be cut up into many smaller sizes, the one of the following that has the LEAST cost per cubic inch of sponge is

   A. 2" x 4" x 6" sponges @ $0.24
   B. 4" x 8" x 12" sponges @ $1.44
   C. 4" x 6" x 36" sponges @ $4.80
   D. 6" x 8" x 32" sponges @ $9.60

   3._____

4. Many new products are used in new schools for floors, walls, and other surfaces. A custodian-engineer should determine the BEST procedure to be used to clean such new surfaces by

   A. referring to the board of education's manual of procedures
   B. obtaining information on the cleaning procedure from the manufacturer
   C. asking the advice of the mechanics who installed the new material
   D. asking the district supervisor how to clean the surfaces

   4._____

5. The one of the following chemicals that a custodian-engineer should tell a cleaner to use to remove mildew from terrazzo is

   A. ammonia              B. oxalic acid
   C. sodium hypochlorite  D. sodium silicate

   5._____

6. The type of soft floor that is basically a mixture of oxidized linseed oil, resin, and ground cork pressed upon a burlap backing is known as

   A. asphalt tile  B. cork tile
   C. linoleum      D. vinyl tile

   6._____

7. The difficulty of cleaning soil from surfaces is LEAST affected by the

   A. length of time between cleanings
   B. chemical nature of the soil

   7._____

C. smoothness of the surface being cleaned
D. standard time allotted to the job

8. The one of the following cleaning agents that is GENERALLY classified as an alkaline cleaner is

   A. sodium carbonate
   B. ground silica
   C. kerosene
   D. lemon oil

9. The one of the following cleaning agents that should be used ONLY when adequate ventilation and protective measures have been taken is

   A. methylene chloride
   B. sodium chloride
   C. sodium carbonate
   D. calcium carbonate

10. Of the following, the MOST important consideration in the selection of a cleaning agent is the

    A. cost per pound or gallon
    B. amount of labor involved in its use
    C. wording of the manufacturer's warranty
    D. length of time the manufacturer has been producing cleaning agents

11. The fan motor in a central vacuum cleaner system is found to be operating at 110% of its rated capacity.
    The one of the following actions which is MOST likely to decrease the load on the motor is

    A. tying-back several outlets in the open position on each floor
    B. moving the butterfly damper slightly toward the closed position
    C. removing ten percent of the filter bags
    D. operating the bag shaker continuously

12. A groundskeeper asks how to remove an accumulation of grease from the concrete near the loading dock.
    Of the following, the cleaning agent that a custodian-engineer should tell him to use to degrease the area is a(n)

    A. acid cleaner
    B. alkaline cleaner
    C. liquid soap
    D. solvent cleaner

13. The instructions for mixing a powdered cleaner in water state, *Mix three ounces of powder in a 14-quart pail three-quarters full of water.*
    A cleaner asks you how much powdered cleaner he should use in a mop truck containing 28 gallons of water to obtain the same strength solution. Your answer should be _____ ounces of powder.

    A. 6
    B. 8
    C. 24
    D. 32

14. A resin-base floor finish USUALLY

    A. gives the highest lustre of all floor finishes
    B. should be applied in one heavy coat
    C. provides a slip-resistant surface
    D. should not be used on asphalt tile

15. The one of the following cleaning operations on soft floors that generally requires MOST NEARLY the same amount of time per 1,000 square feet as damp mopping is

    A. applying a thin coat of wax
    B. sweeping
    C. dust mopping
    D. wet mopping

16. Of the following cleaning jobs, the one that should be allowed the MOST time to complete a 1,000 square foot area is

    A. vacuuming carpets
    B. washing painted walls
    C. stripping and waxing soft floors
    D. machine-scrubbing hard floors

17. When instructing your staff in the use of sodium silicate, you should tell them that it is MOST commonly used to

    A. seal concrete floors
    B. condition leather
    C. treat boiler water
    D. neutralize acid wastes

18. Cleaners should be instructed that dust mopping is LEAST appropriate for removing light soil from _____ floors.

    A. terrazzo
    B. unsealed concrete
    C. resin-finished soft
    D. sealed wood

19. Of the following, the substance that should be recommended for polishing hardwood furniture is

    A. lemon oil polish
    B. neat's-foot oil
    C. paste wax
    D. water-emulsion wax

20. The use of concentrated acid to remove stains from ceramic tile bathroom floors USUALLY results in making the surface

    A. pitted and porous
    B. clean and shiny
    C. harder and glossier
    D. waterproof

21. Asphalt tile floors should be protected by coating them with

    A. hard-milled soap
    B. water-emulsion wax
    C. sodium metaphosphate
    D. varnish

22. Of the following, the BEST way to economize on cleaning tools and materials is to

    A. train the cleaners to use them properly
    B. order at least a three-year supply of every item in order to avpid annual price increases
    C. attach a price sticker to every item so that the people using them will realize their high cost
    D. delay ordering material for three months at the beginning of each year to be sure that the old material is used to the fullest extent

23. The MINIMUM amount of free chlorine that swimming pool water should contain for proper disinfection is _____ parts per million.

    A. 1.0   B. 10   C. 50   D. 500

24. The point at which swimming pool filters should be back-washed is when the difference between the inlet and outlet pressures EXCEEDS _____ psi.

    A. 5   B. 10   C. 15   D. 20

25. An orthotolidine test is used to test a water sample to see what quantity it contains of

    A. alum   B. ammonia   C. chlorine   D. soda ash

26. The ideal flue gas temperature in a rotary-cup oil-fired boiler should be equal to the steam temperature PLUS

    A. 50° F   B. 125° F   C. 275° F   D. 550° F

27. The carbon dioxide reading in a boiler flue when the boiler is operating efficiently should be MOST NEARLY

    A. 0.5 inches of water
    B. 8 ounces per mol
    C. 10 psi
    D. 12 percent

28. The one of the following that PRIMARILY indicates a low water level in a steam boiler is the

    A. pressure gauge
    B. gauge glass
    C. safety valve
    D. hydrometer

29. The one of the following steps that should be taken FIRST if a safety valve on a coal-fired steam boiler pops off is to

    A. add water to the boiler
    B. reduce the draft
    C. tap the side of the safety valve with a mallet
    D. open the bottom blow-off valve

30. A device that operates to vary the resistance of an electrical circuit is USUALLY part of a _____ pressurtrol.

    A. high-limit
    B. low-limit
    C. manual-reset
    D. modulating

# KEY (CORRECT ANSWERS)

| | | | |
|---|---|---|---|
| 1. | C | 16. | C |
| 2. | A | 17. | A |
| 3. | B | 18. | B |
| 4. | B | 19. | C |
| 5. | C | 20. | A |
| 6. | C | 21. | B |
| 7. | D | 22. | A |
| 8. | A | 23. | A |
| 9. | A | 24. | B |
| 10. | B | 25. | C |
| 11. | B | 26. | B |
| 12. | D | 27. | D |
| 13. | D | 28. | B |
| 14. | C | 29. | B |
| 15. | A | 30. | D |

———

# TEST 2

DIRECTIONS: Each question or incomplete statement is followed by several suggested answers or completions. Select the one that BEST answers the question or completes the statement. *PRINT THE LETTER OF THE CORRECT ANSWER IN THE SPACE AT THE RIGHT.*

1. A solenoid valve is actuated by

    A. air pressure
    B. electric current
    C. temperature change
    D. light rays

    1.___

2. A sequential draft control on a rotary-cup oil-fired boiler should operate to

    A. *open* the automatic damper at the end of the post-purge period
    B. *open* the automatic damper when the draft has increased during normal burner operation
    C. *close* the automatic damper just before the burner motor starts up
    D. *close* the automatic damper after the burner goes off and the burner cycle is completed

    2.___

3. The one of the following components of flue gas that indicates, when present, that more excess air is being supplied than is being used is

    A. carbon dioxide
    B. carbon monoxide
    C. nitrogen
    D. oxygen

    3.___

4. An advantage that a float-thermostatic steam trap has over a float-type steam trap of comparable rating is that a float-thermostatic trap

    A. requires less maintenance
    B. is easier to install
    C. allows non-condensable gases to escape
    D. releases the condensate at a higher temperature

    4.___

5. A pump delivers 165 pounds of water per minute against a total head of 100 feet. The water horsepower of this pump is _____ HP.

    A. 1/2   B. 2   C. 5   D. 20

    5.___

6. Of the following, the BEST instrument to use to measure over-the-fire draft is the

    A. Bourdon tube gauge
    B. inclined manometer
    C. mercury manometer
    D. potentiometer

    6.___

7. The temperature of the water in a steam-heated domestic hot water tank is controlled by a(n)

    A. aquastat
    B. thermostatic regulating valve
    C. vacuum breaker
    D. thermostatic trap

    7.___

8. The one of the following conditions that will MOST likely cause fuel oil pressure to fluctuate is

    A. a faulty pressure gauge
    B. a clean oil-strainer
    C. cold oil in the suction line
    D. an over-tight pump drive belt

    8.___

9. The cooler in a Freon 12 refrigeration system that is equipped with automatic protective devices is MOST likely to be accidentally damaged by water freeze-up when the system('s)

    A. is operating at reduced load
    B. is operating at rated load
    C. condenser water-flow is interrupted
    D. is being pumped down

10. The capacity of a water-cooled condenser is LEAST affected by the

    A. water temperature
    B. refrigerant temperature
    C. surrounding air temperature
    D. quantity of condenser water being circulated

11. Of the following chemicals used in boiler feedwater treatment, the one that should be used to RETARD corrosion in the boiler circuit due to dissolved oxygen is sodium

    A. aluminate    B. carbonate    C. phosphate    D. sulfite

12. The heating system in a certain school is equipped with vacuum return condensate pumps.
    The MOST likely place for an air-vent valve to be installed in this plant is on

    A. each radiator
    B. the outlet of the domestic hot water steam heating coil
    C. the pressure side of the vacuum pump
    D. the shell of the domestic hot water tank

13. *Priming* of a steam boiler is NOT caused by

    A. load swings
    B. uneven fire distribution
    C. too high a water level
    D. high alkalinity of the boiler water

14. A Hartford loop is used in school heating systems PRIMARILY to

    A. provide for thermal expansion of the steam distribution piping
    B. equalize the water level in two or more boilers
    C. prevent siphoning of water out of the boiler
    D. by-pass the electric fuel-oil heaters when the steam heaters are operating

15. Of the following, the MOST likely use for temperature-indicating crayons by a custodian-engineer is in

    A. checking the operation of the radiator traps
    B. replacing room thermometers that have been vandalized
    C. indicating possible sources of spontaneous combustion
    D. checking the effectiveness of an insulating panel

16. A stop-and-waste cock is GENERALLY used on

   A. refrigerant lines between the compressor and the condenser
   B. soil lines
   C. gas supply lines
   D. water lines subjected to low temperatures

17. A pressure-regulating valve in a compressed air line should be preceded by a(n)

   A. check valve           B. intercooler
   C. needle valve          D. water-and-oil separator

18. A house trap is a fitting placed in the house drain immediately inside the foundation wall of a building.
    The MAIN purpose of a house trap is to

   A. prevent the entrance of sewer gas into the building drainage system
   B. provide access to the drain lines in the basement for cleaning
   C. drain the basement in case of flooding
   D. maintain balanced air pressure in the fixture traps

19. The one of the following that is BEST to use to smooth a commutator is

   A. Number 1/0 emery cloth     B. Number 00 sandpaper
   C. Number 2 steel wool        D. a safe edge file

20. The electric service that is provided to MOST schools in the city is NOMINALLY

   A. 208 volt-3 phase -4 wire - 120 volts to ground
   B. 208 volt-3 phase -3 wire - 208 volts to ground
   C. 220 volt-2 phase -3 wire - 110 volts to ground
   D. 440 volt-3 phase -4 wire - 240 volts to ground

21. All the fuses in an electrical panel are good but the clips on the fuse in circuit No. 1 are much hotter than the clips of the other fuses.
    Of the following, the MOST likely cause of this condition is that

   A. circuit No. 1 is greatly overloaded
   B. circuit No. 1 is carrying much less than rated load
   C. the room temperature is abnormally high
   D. the fuse in circuit No. 1 is very loose in its clips

22. Of the following, the BEST tool to use to drive a lag screw is a(n)

   A. open-end wrench       B. Stillson wrench
   C. screwdriver           D. alien wrench

23. Of the following, the one that is MOST likely to be used in landscaping work as ground cover is

   A. Barberry              B. Forsythia
   C. Pachysandra           D. Viburnum

24. The velocity of air in a ventilation duct is USUALLY measured with a(n)

   A. hydrometer            B. psychrometer
   C. pyrometer             D. pitot tube

25. The motor driving a centrifugal pump through a direct-connected flexible coupling burned out.
   When a new motor is ordered, it is important to specify the same NEMA frame size so that the

   A. horsepower will be the same
   B. speed will be the same
   C. conduit box will be in the same location
   D. mounting dimensions will be the same

26. A custodian-engineer should inspect the school building for safety

   A. at least once each day
   B. at least every other day
   C. at least once a week
   D. at the end of each vacation period

27. Of the following, the MOST important practice to follow in order to prevent fires in a school is to train the staff to

   A. fight fires of every kind
   B. detect and eliminate every possible fire hazard
   C. keep halls, corridors, and exits clear
   D. place flammables in fire-proof containers

28. The one of the following types of portable fire extinguishers that is MOST effective in fighting an oil fire is the _____ type.

   A. soda-acid           B. loaded-stream
   C. foam                D. carbon dioxide

29. A custodian-engineer opens the door to the boiler room and discovers that fuel oil has leaked onto the floor and caught fire.
   Of the following, the FIRST action he should take is to

   A. notify the Principal
   B. notify the fire department
   C. turn off the remote control switch
   D. fight the fire using a Class B extinguisher

30. The MINIMUM noise level beyond which hearing may be impaired is _____ decibels.

   A. 10          B. 50          C. 90          D. 130

# KEY (CORRECT ANSWERS)

| | | | |
|---|---|---|---|
| 1. | B | 16. | D |
| 2. | D | 17. | D |
| 3. | D | 18. | A |
| 4. | C | 19. | B |
| 5. | A | 20. | A |
| 6. | B | 21. | D |
| 7. | B | 22. | A |
| 8. | C | 23. | C |
| 9. | D | 24. | D |
| 10. | C | 25. | D |
| 11. | D | 26. | A |
| 12. | B | 27. | B |
| 13. | D | 28. | C |
| 14. | C | 29. | C |
| 15. | A | 30. | C |

# EXAMINATION SECTION
# TEST 1

DIRECTIONS: Each question or incomplete statement is followed by several suggested answers or completions. Select the one that BEST answers the question or completes the statement. *PRINT THE LETTER OF THE CORRECT ANSWER IN THE SPACE AT THE RIGHT.*

1. A boiler horse power is defined as the evaporation of _____ pounds of water per hour, from and at, 212° F.

    A. 32.0  B. 14.7  C. 34.5  D. 29.9

    1._____

2. The steam drum of a water tube boiler is 16 feet long and 42" in diameter. Assuming that the normal water line is at the drum centerline, the water content of the drum under normal operating conditions is *most nearly*

    A. 700 gallons
    B. 600 gallons
    C. 400 gallons
    D. 400 cubic feet

    2._____

3. In selecting a coal from its "Proximate Analysis," which of the following coals would you consider to be best suited for use in a boiler plant in a heavily populated city?

    A. 7% ash - 18% volatile matter
    B. 10% ash - 21% volatile matter
    C. 12% ash - 17% volatile matter
    D. 5% ash - 25% volatile matter

    3._____

4. Which of the following types of grates should be used for ease in cleaning fires, when hand-firing large boilers with #1 buckwheat, under natural draft at heavy loads?

    A. Dumping grates
    B. Stationary grates with 3/4" air spaces
    C. Stationary grates (pin hole type)
    D. Shaking grates

    4._____

5. Which of the following fuels contains the *greatest* number of heat units per pound?

    A. Hard coal
    B. No. 6 Fuel Oil
    C. Yard screenings
    D. Bituminous coal

    5._____

6. In the usual water tube boiler plant using coal under natural draft, the point where the *maximum* negative draft gauge reading may be obtained is

    A. at the top of the stack
    B. at the base of the stack
    C. over the fire
    D. in the last pass

    6._____

2 (#1)

7. The purpose of admitting air over the fire in a coal-fired furnace is *usually* to

   A. reduce the stack gas temperature
   B. improve the draft
   C. reduce the smoke
   D. reduce the draft

8. With steam at a temperature of 365° F in a boiler, which of the following stack gas temperatures would you consider to be *good* usual operating practice in a plant without economizers, air preheaters and the like?

   A. 300° F  B. 500° F  C. 700° F  D. 900° F

9. The percentage of $CO_2$ in the stack gases is an indication of the

   A. rate of combustion in the furnace
   B. rate at which excess air is supplied to the furnace
   C. rate of carbon monoxide production in the furnace
   D. temperature of combustion

10. In the most usual type of large capacity oil burner using #6 oil, under "fully automatic" control, the atomization of the oil is produced MAINLY by the

    A. pressure from the pump
    B. pressure from the secondary air fan
    C. oil temperature from the heater
    D. rotation of the burner assembly by the motor

11. Of the following, the figure which comes the *closest* to indicating the number of degree days in a normal heating season in New York City is

    A. 3000  B. 4000  C. 5000  D. 6000

12. In which of the following steam generation methods would you expect to obtain reasonably continuous values of $CO_2$ *closest* to the perfect $CO_2$ value?

    A. Automatic stoker firing with temperature recorder
    B. Automatic stoker firing with "Hold fire timer"
    C. Automatic oil firing with "Stack switch"
    D. Automatic oil firing with "haze regulator"

13. The loss of heat in stack gases for heavy fuel oil is HIGHEST when the

    A. $CO_2$ content is 12% and the stack temperature is 500°
    B. $CO_2$ content is 8% and the stack temperature is 600°
    C. $CO_2$ content is 6% and the stack temperature is 700°
    D. $CO_2$ content is 14% and the stack temperature is 600°

14. A badly sooted HRT boiler under coal firing will show

    A. a higher $CO_2$ value than a clean boiler
    B. a lower $CO_2$ value than a clean boiler

C. a higher stack temperature than a clean boiler
D. a lower draft loss than a clean boiler

15. A unit heater condensing 50 lbs. of low pressure steam per hour would be rated *most nearly* at _____ square feet E.D.R.

    A. 50   B. 100   C. 150   D. 200

16. One horsepower most nearly equals

    A. 550 ft - lbs per sec.
    B. 3300 ft - lbs per min.
    C. 55000 ft - lbs per hour
    D. 10000 ft-lbs per min.

17. An indicator card from a steam engine is MOST useful to the custodian-engineer in

    A. determining the boiler pressure
    B. determining the engine speed
    C. adjusting the valve setting
    D. computing the mechanical efficiency

18. Which one of the following statements is *most nearly* correct?

    A. A water tube boiler has the combustion gases inside the tubes
    B. A scotch marine boiler has two drums
    C. A brick set HRT boiler usually has a steel fire box
    D. The circulation in a boiler may be either gravity or forced

19. When the load on a mechanical stoker fired boiler plant furnishing steam for slide valve engine generators drops by 30%, the

    A. stoker should be shut down
    B. fan should be speeded up and the stoker slowed
    C. stoker should be speeded up and the air supply reduced
    D. stoker speed and air supply should be adjusted by reducing both

20. Which of the following statements is *most nearly* correct?

    A. All types of mechanical stokers may be used with equal efficiency under all types of boilers
    B. Most stokers are designed with a weak member
    C. The best type of stoker to use is not dependent upon the type of fuel available
    D. Advisability of installing stokers is not dependent upon the load

21. The number and size of safety valves required on a high pressure boiler is dependent upon the

    A. size of the boiler drums
    B. amount of heating surface
    C. number of pounds of fuel burned per square foot of grate per hour
    D. size of the steam main

22. In changing over a boiler from high pressure (150 lbs. per square inch) to 10 pounds per square inch, it is usually necessary to

    A. increase the size of the safety valves
    B. decrease the grate area
    C. increase the size of the feed water piping
    D. increase the size of the blow down piping

23. A boiler feed injector becomes temporarily steam bound. To correct this condition, the MOST proper action to take is to

    A. increase boiler pressure
    B. reduce suction lift
    C. wrap it with cold rags
    D. bank fire

24. If the volume of air in cubic feet per minute for combustion is represented by X, which of the following values of X would *most nearly* represent the Cfm of stack gas, under usual conditions, that an induced draft fan would have to handle?

    A. X  B. 2X  C. 3X  D. 4X

25. If the stock switch of an oil burner becomes excessively sooted, a condition *most likely* to result is

    A. continuous shutting down of the burner shortly after it starts up
    B. excessive flow of oil to the burner resulting in a smoky fire
    C. excessive fire due to failure to cut off current to the burner motor
    D. failure of the warp switch of the relay to operate

## KEY (CORRECT ANSWERS)

| | | | |
|---|---|---|---|
| 1. | C | 11. | C |
| 2. | B | 12. | D |
| 3. | A | 13. | C |
| 4. | A | 14. | C |
| 5. | B | 15. | D |
| 6. | B | 16. | A |
| 7. | C | 17. | C |
| 8. | B | 18. | D |
| 9. | B | 19. | D |
| 10. | D | 20. | B |

21. B
22. A
23. C
24. B
25. A

# TEST 2

DIRECTIONS: Each question or incomplete statement is followed by several suggested answers or completions. Select the one that BEST answers the question or completes the statement. *PRINT THE LETTER OF THE CORRECT ANSWER IN THE SPACE AT THE RIGHT.*

1. In high pressure electric generating plants in large buildings, heating the feed water from 70° F to 180° F with exhaust steam usually will *decrease* the fuel consumption by

   A. 5%    B. 10%    C. 15%    D. 20%

2. The direct room radiator with a pneumatically controlled steam heating system is cold, while the adjoining rooms are heated adequately.
   Of the following, the FIRST thing you would check in the room is the

   A. steam pipe in the room before the pneumatic steam valve
   B. thermostat
   C. pneumatic steam valve
   D. thermostatic trap

3. The usual vacuum gage on a steam heating system reads in

   A. inches of vacuum
   B. feet of mercury
   C. inches of water
   D. feet of water

4. In a mechanical pressure type burner using #6 oil heated to 230°F by steam, the oil is atomized by

   A. centrifugal force
   B. steam temperature
   C. oil temperature
   D. oil pressure

5. A vaporstat with separate motor driven oil pump used on a fully automatic heavy oil burning rotary cup installation is *generally* used to

   A. keep the boiler pressure within proper limits
   B. regulate the pressure of the primary air
   C. regulate the pressure of the secondary air
   D. shut down the burner when primary air failure occurs

6. In estimating the amount of work being done by a steam driven water pump, the one of the following items which is usually the MOST important in the calculation of pump horsepower is the

   A. temperature of the water
   B. suction lift
   C. steam pressure
   D. gallons pumped

37

7. The term "fixture unit" *usually* refers to

   A. the number of lamp sockets in an electric lighting fixture
   B. the number of fixtures in a room or building
   C. a rate of flow
   D. amperes per second

8. When pumping water from a return tank, equipped with an automatic make up valve located below the pump, the *most probable* cause of periodic pump failures to deliver the water, would be

   A. a leak in the suction line
   B. the water was too hot
   C. there was too much water in the tank
   D. a leak in the discharge line

9. Suppose a small oil fire has broken out in the boiler room in your building. Under these circumstances, the extinguisher LEAST suitable for use is

   A. soda-acid            B. pyrene
   C. foamite              D. carbon dioxide

10. Of the following, a low "power factor" would MOST likely result from:

    A. Corlis valve engine operating at less than 1/2 normal rated load
    B. A large d.c. motor operating at 20% below normal speed
    C. A large induction motor operating at 60% normal rated capacity
    D. A storage battery on which the voltage has dropped to 10% below normal

11. Before putting two d.c. engine generators on the line in parallel, it is usually necessary to

    A. adjust the speeds so that both are running at exactly the same speed
    B. adjust the loads so that each machine will take its proportionate share
    C. adjust the field of the incoming unit
    D. lower the line voltage

12. Of the following, the BEST type of AC motor to use for direct connection to a timing device which must be very accurate is a

    A. synchronous motor
    B. squirrel cage motor
    C. wound rotor motor
    D. single phase capacitor motor

13. In running temporary electric wiring for a display requiring the use of 30 incandescent 50-watt lamps at the usual lighting voltage, the two main 120V loads supplying this load would carry *most nearly* _____ amps.

    A. 23.9        B. 12.5        C. 17.8        D. 9.5

14. One ton of refrigeration may be expressed MOST accurately as

    A. one ton of ice melting per hour      B. 200 Btu per minute
    C. one horsepower-hour                  D. 970 Btu per pound

15. Which of the following statements is correct with respect to filtration plants of swimming pools:

    A. In pressure filter installations a clear well tank is always required as a reservoir of filtered water
    B. Raw water should be used to backwash filters whenever possible
    C. The rate of backwashing usually is less than the rate of filtration
    D. Alum is added to water to form a flee before the water reaches the filters

15._____

16. In the operation of a swimming pool, the statement NOT true is:

    A. All water supplied must be sterilized at the plant by chemical means
    B. The pool must be cleaned every third time that it is drained
    C. The rate of recirculation is dependent upon the size of the pool
    D. The number of persons permitted to use the pool at any one time determines the rate of recirculation

16._____

17. Of the following, the use for which central vacuum cleaning is considered LEAST effective is for

    A. cleaning walls and ceilings
    B. dusting classroom furniture
    C. cleaning boiler rooms
    D. cleaning erasers

17._____

18. An electric elevator car stalls on the ground floor of a school building. Of the following, the item you would be LEAST likely to check in your inspection is the

    A. "baby" switch
    B. floor door switch
    C. limit switch
    D. current to elevator motors

18._____

19. An examination of the water supply of the sinks of demonstration tables in science rooms reveals the use of rubber hose attachments to sink taps extending below the sink rim. Of the following, the MOST important criticism of this practice is that

    A. there is greater possibility of water waste through leakage
    B. the taps may become contaminated by contact with unclean rubber hoses
    C. a submerged inlet condition may be created resulting in back-siphonage
    D. a water hammer condition will be created by this elimination of the normal air gap

19._____

20. In an investigation of a complaint of sewer gas from a urinal in a regularly used toilet room, you find that the trap seal has been lost. The LEAST common cause of this condition is

    A. evaporation of water from the trap
    B. vents blocked up
    C. high wind over roof vent
    D. self-siphonage

20._____

21. A *check* valve in the discharge of a centrifugal pump 21.____

   A. prevents backflow to suction side
   B. keeps the pump primed at all times
   C. eliminates the need for a foot valve
   D. eliminates the need for a gate valve on the pump discharge

22. The modern multiple-circuit program instrument which automatically controls bell signals in a school *usually* includes 22.____

   A. automatic resetting of electric clocks throughout the school
   B. automatic ringing of room bells when the fire bell switch is closed
   C. prevention of manual control of schedules by eliminating manual control switches
   D. provision for automatic cutout of the schedule for any 24-hour day desired

23. Of the following, the cleaning assignment which you would LEAST prefer to have performed *during* school hours is 23.____

   A. sweeping of corridors and stairs
   B. cleaning and polishing brass fixtures
   C. cleaning toilets
   D. dusting of offices, halls and special rooms

24. A mechanical system of ventilation commonly found in schools is a unit ventilator (univent) located in each classroom. Of the following, the procedure which is NOT usually correct with respect to operation and maintenance of this unit is 24.____

   A. air pressure for operation of the unit is obtained from a central fan located in the basement
   B. when a room is to be heated in the early morning of a cold day by recirculation, the window is closed and the damper opened to the room
   C. filters coated with oil are periodically cleaned by dipping them in a solution of washing soda and hot water
   D. other radiators in the room are not normally controlled by the univent or its radiator

25. A teacher complains to you that her room is not cleaned properly each day. You have received complaints from this teacher on several occasions and have found them to be unfounded each time. The *most desirable* action to take is to FIRST 25.____

   A. tell the teacher that her room is cleaned as well as other rooms
   B. advise the teacher that she is expecting too much of the custodial staff
   C. ask the cleaner if he cleans that classroom in accordance with standard procedures
   D. visit the room to verify the complaint of the teacher

## KEY (CORRECT ANSWERS)

1. B
2. A
3. A
4. D
5. D

6. D
7. C
8. B
9. A
10. C

11. C
12. A
13. B
14. B
15. D

16. B
17. B
18. C
19. C
20. A

21. A
22. A
23. D
24. A
25. D

# EXAMINATION SECTION
# TEST 1

DIRECTIONS: Each question or incomplete statement is followed by several suggested answers or completions. Select the one that BEST answers the question or completes the statement. *PRINT THE LETTER OF THE CORRECT ANSWER IN THE SPACE AT THE RIGHT.*

1. The KEY figure in any custodial safety program is the  1.____
   A. custodian    B. cleaner    C. mayor    D. commissioner

2. A custodian must inspect or have a maintenance man inspect every window cleaner's safety belt AT LEAST  2.____
   A. each time the windows are washed
   B. once a month
   C. once a year
   D. once every second year

3. A custodian's written instruction to his staff on the subject of security in public buildings should include instructions to  3.____
   A. exclude the public at all times
   B. admit the public at all times
   C. admit the public only if they are neat and well-dressed
   D. admit the public during specified hours

4. A custodian in charge of a building who is normally on duty during the daytime hours in a building which is cleaned at night should  4.____
   A. never make night inspections since he is not responsible for the cleanliness of the building
   B. make night inspections at least once a year
   C. never make night inspections because the cleaners will think he is spying on them
   D. make night inspections at least twice a month

5. The employee MOST likely to find the nests and runways in a building of roaches and vermin is a  5.____
   A. maintenance man    B. building custodian
   C. night cleaner    D. stationary fireman

6. When mopping, the pails containing the cleaning solutions should be  6.____
   A. slid along the floor to avoid injury due to lifting
   B. kept off the floor, preferably on a rolling platform
   C. shifted from place to place using a mop
   D. equipped with a spigot for applying the mopping solution

7. Of the following, the item that is considered a concrete floor sealer is
   A. water wax
   B. sodium hypochlorite
   C. sodium silicate
   D. linseed oil

8. A material COMMONLY used in detergent is
   A. rock salt
   B. Glauber's salt
   C. tri-sodium phosphate
   D. monosodium glutamate

9. A disinfectant material is one that will
   A. kill germs
   B. dissolve soil and stop odors
   C. give a clean odor and cover a disagreeable odor
   D. prevent soil buildup

10. When scrubbing a wooden floor, it is ADVISABLE to
    A. flood the surface with the cleaning solution in order to float the soil out of all crevices
    B. hose off the loosened soil before starting the scrubbing operation
    C. pick up the used solution as soon as possible
    D. mix a mild acid with the cleaning solution in order to clean the surface quickly

11. Before starting a wall washing operation, it is BEST to
    A. check the temperature of the water
    B. soak the sponge to be used
    C. check the pH of the mixed cleaning solution
    D. dust the wall to be washed

12. Of the following, the MOST nearly correct statement regarding the economical operation of the heating system in a building is that
    A. the heat should always be shut down at 4 P.M. and turned on at 8 A.M.
    B. the heat should be shut down only over the weekend
    C. it is best to keep the heat on at all times so that the number of complaints are kept to a minimum
    D. the times at which the heat is shut down and turned on should be varied depending on the prevailing outdoor temperature

13. A floor made of marble or granite chis imbedded in cement is USUALLY called
    A. terrazzo   B. linoleum   C. palmetto   D. parquet

14. In a 4-wire, 3-phase electrical supply system, the voltage between one phase and ground used for the lighting is MOST NEARLY
    A. 440   B. 230   C. 208   D. 115

15. Of the following, the one that takes the place of a fuse in an electrical circuit is a
    A. transformer
    B. circuit breaker
    C. condenser
    D. knife switch

16. Gas bills are USUALLY computed on the basis of
    A. cubic feet    B. gallons    C. pounds    D. kilowatts

17. An operating oil-fired steam boiler explosion may sometimes be caused by
    A. carrying too high a water level in the boiler
    B. inadequate purging of combustion chamber between fires
    C. overfiring the boiler
    D. carrying too high an oil temperature

18. The one of the following commercial sizes of anthracite which is the LARGEST in size is
    A. stove    B. chestnut    C. pea    D. rice

19. Assume that six windows of a public building facing one street have been consistently broken by boys playing ball after hours and over weekends.
    The BEST solution to this problem is to
    A. post a no ball playing sign on the wall
    B. erect protective screening outside the six windows
    C. post a guard on weekend patrol duty
    D. request special weekend police protection for the property

20. The BEST method or tool to use for cleaning dust from an unplastered cinder-block wall is
    A. a Tampico brush with stock cleaning solution
    B. a vacuum cleaner
    C. water under pressure from hose and nozzle
    D. a feather duster

21. Of the following, the LARGEST individual item of expense in operating a public building is generally the cost of
    A. cleaning                B. heating fuel
    C. electricity             D. elevator service

22. The CHIEF purpose for changing the handle of a floor brush from one side of the brush block to the other side is to
    A. allow the janitor to change hands
    B. make both sides of the brush equally dirty
    C. give both sides of the brush equal wear
    D. change the angle of sweeping

23. Of the following, the weight of mop MOST likely used in the nightly mopping of corridors, halls, or lobbies is _____ ounce.
    A. 8    B. 16    C. 24    D. 50

24. After sweeping assignment is completed, floor brushes should be stored
    A. in a pan of water
    B. by hanging the brushes on pegs or nails
    C. by piling the brushes on each other carefully
    D. in a normal sweeping position, bristles resting on the floor

25. Nylon-treated scrubbing discs
    A. require more water than scrubbing brushes
    B. require more detergent solution than scrubbing brushes
    C. must be used with cold water only
    D. are generally more effective than steel wool pads

26. Of the following, the BEST material to use to clean exterior bronze is
    A. pumice             B. paste wax
    C. wire wheel on portable buffer    D. lemon oil polish

27. The use of trisodium phosphate in cleaning polished marble should be AVOIDED because it
    A. may cause spalling
    B. discolors the surface of the marble
    C. builds up a slick surface on the marble
    D. pits the glazed surface and bleaches the marble

28. The floor area, in square feet, on which a properly treated dustless sweeping cloth can be used before the cloth must be washed is
    A. 500-1000   B. 2000-3000   C. 4000-6000   D. 8000-10000

29. A cleaning woman working a six-hour shift should be able to cover (clean) _____ Gilbert work units.
    A. 100-200   B. 400-500   C. 1100-1200   D. 6000-7000

30. An incipient fire is one which
    A. has just started and can be readily extinguished using an ordinary hand extinguisher
    B. occurs only in motor vehicles
    C. is burning out of control in a storeroom
    D. is a banked coal fire

31. Maintaining room temperature at 75°F in the winter time will increase fuel consumption above the amount needed to maintain 70°F by APPROXIMATELY
    A. 5%   B. 10%   C. 15%   D. 20%

32. Of the following, the one which represents the BEST practical combustion condition in an oil-fired low pressure steam plant is _____ stack temperature.
    A. 8% $CO_2$ - 500°F        B. 13% $CO_2$ - 400°F
    C. 10% $CO_2$ - 700°F       D. 6% $CO_2$ - 400°F

33. An office has floor dimensions of 6 ft. 6 in. wide by 22 ft. 0 in. long. The floor area of this office, in square feet, is MOST NEARLY
    A. 143   B. 263   C. 363   D. 463

34. Dollies are USUALLY used
    A. as convenient platforms upon which to store items
    B. as ornamental protective covers

C. to raise items to the required level
D. to transport items from one place to another

35. When lifting a heavy object from a table, which of the following rules is it MOST important to observe?
    A. Do not bend your knees.
    B. Do not stand too close to the object.
    C. Keep your back straight.
    D. Keep your shoulder level with the object

36. The FIRST objective of all fire prevention is
    A. confining fire to a limited area
    B. safeguarding life against fire
    C. reducing insurance rates
    D. preventing property damage

37. A custodian should know the equipment used in his work well enough to
    A. make any repairs which might be needed
    B. know what parts to remove in case of breakdown
    C. anticipate any reasonable possibility of a breakdown
    D. know all the lubricants specified by the manufacturer

38. The PRIMARY responsibility of a supervising custodian is to
    A. make friends of all subordinates
    B. search for new methods of doing the work
    C. win the respect of his superior
    D. get the work done properly within a reasonable time

39. When a custodian believes that the work of a subordinate is below standard, he should
    A. assign the employee to work that is considered undesirable
    B. do nothing immediately in the hope that the employee will bring his work up to standard without any help from the supervisor
    C. reduce the privileges of the employee at once
    D. discuss it as soon as possible with the employee

40. An office worker frequently complains to the custodian that her office is poorly illuminated.
    The BEST action for the custodian to follow is to
    A. ignore the complaints as those of an habitual crank
    B. inform the worker that illumination is a fixed item built into the building originally and evidently is the result of faulty planning by the architect
    C. request a licensed electrician to install additional ceiling lights
    D. investigate for faulty illumination features in the room, such as dirty lamp globes and incorrect lamp wattages

## KEY (CORRECT ANSWERS)

| | | | | | | | |
|---|---|---|---|---|---|---|---|
| 1. | A | 11. | D | 21. | A | 31. | D |
| 2. | C | 12. | D | 22. | C | 32. | B |
| 3. | D | 13. | A | 23. | C | 33. | C |
| 4. | D | 14. | D | 24. | B | 34. | D |
| 5. | B | 15. | B | 25. | D | 35. | C |
| 6. | B | 16. | A | 26. | D | 36. | B |
| 7. | C | 17. | B | 27. | A | 37. | C |
| 8. | C | 18. | A | 28. | C | 38. | D |
| 9. | A | 19. | B | 29. | C | 39. | D |
| 10. | C | 20. | B | 30. | A | 40. | D |

# TEST 2

DIRECTIONS: Each question or incomplete statement is followed by several suggested answers or completions. Select the one that BEST answers the question or completes the statement. *PRINT THE LETTER OF THE CORRECT ANSWER IN THE SPACE AT THE RIGHT.*

1. Of the following, the MOST important reason for the custodian to plan work schedules for men under his supervision is that
    A. emergency situations can easily be handled if they should arise
    B. it insures that essential operations will be adequately covered
    C. the men will be more satisfied if a routine is established
    D. the relationship between the supervisor and his subordinate will be clarified

2. Sealers for open-grained wood floors should NOT contain linseed oil because
    A. the linseed oil would damage the wood fibers
    B. the linseed oil would deteriorate mop strands
    C. water wax would penetrate the linseed oil sealer and rot the wood
    D. linseed oil on wood take too long to dry satisfactorily before a floor finish could be applied

3. When washing painted wall areas by hand, a man should be expected to wash each hour an area, in square feet, equal to
    A. 75-125    B. 150-300    C. 400-600    D. 750-1000

4. Of the following, the one that is MOST desirable to use in dusting furniture is a
    A. feather duster              B. paper towel
    C. counter brush               D. soft cotton cloth

5. The one of the following floor types on which oily sweeping compound may be used is
    A. vinyl tile    B. concrete    C. linoleum    D. terrazzo

6. A steam heating system where the steam and condensate flow in the same pipe is called a _____ system.
    A. one pipe gravity return     B. sub-atmospheric
    C. vacuum return               D. zone control

7. A test of a boiler by applying pressure equal to or greater than the maximum working pressure is called a ____ test.
    A. hydrostatic    B. barometric    C. hygroscopic    D. gyroscopic

8. A stack switch, as used with an oil burner,
    A. shuts down the burner in case of non-ignition
    B. shuts down the burner in case of high stack temperatures
    C. controls the flow of secondary air
    D. operates the barometric damper

9. The vertical pipes leading from the steam mains to the radiators are called
   A. drip lines
   B. risers
   C. radiant coils
   D. expansion joints

10. Fuel oil storage tanks are equipped with vents.
    The purpose of these vents is to
    A. make tank soundings
    B. check oil flash points
    C. fill the fuel tanks
    D. allow air to mix

11. A compound gauge in a boiler room
    A. measures steam and water pressure
    B. shows the quantity of boiler treatment compound on hand
    C. measures pressures above and below atmospheric pressure
    D. indicates the degree of compounding in a steam engine

12. Of the following, the CHIEF purpose of insulating steam lines is to
    A. prevent loss of heat
    B. protect people from being burned by them
    C. prevent leaks
    D. protect the pipes against corrosion

13. The MOST important function of thermostatic traps on radiators is to
    A. regulate the heat given off by the radiators
    B. remove water and air from the radiator
    C. assist the steam pressure in filling the radiator
    D. maintain a vacuum within the radiator

14. The designation *1/8-27N.P.T.* USUALLY indicates
    A. machine screw thread
    B. pipe thread
    C. spur gear size
    D. sprocket chain size

15. The size of a chisel is determined by its
    A. length    B. width    C. pitch    D. height

16. The cause of paint blisters is USUALLY
    A. moisture under the paint coat
    B. too thick a coat of paint
    C. too much oil in paint
    D. the plaster pores not sealed properly

17. A wood-framed picture is to be attached to a plaster and hollow tile wall.
    Of the following, the PROPER installation would include the use of
    A. wire cut nails
    B. miracle glue
    C. expansion shields and screws
    D. self-tapping screws

18. The PROPER tool or method to use for driving a finish nail to the depth necessary for putting when installing wood trim is
    A. countersink
    B. another nail of the same diameter
    C. a nail set
    D. a center punch

19. Faucet leakage in a large building is BEST controlled by periodic
    A. faucet replacement
    B. addition of a sealing compound to the water supply
    C. packing replacement
    D. faucet inspection and repair

20. Escutcheons are USUALLY located
    A. on kitchen cabinet drawers
    B. on windows
    C. around pipes, to cover pipe sleeve openings
    D. around armored electric cable going into a gem box

21. It is ADVISABLE to remove broken bulbs from light sockets with
    A. a wooden or hard rubber wedge
    B. pliers
    C. a hammer and chisel
    D. a fuse puller

22. A room 20' x 25' in area with a ceiling height of 9'6" is to be painted. One gallon of paint will cover 400 square feet.
    The MINIMUM number of gallons necessary to give the four walls and the ceiling one coat of paint is
    A. 2      B. 3      C. 4      D. 5

23. Of the following, the ones on which gaskets are MOST likely to be used are
    A. threaded pipe plugs           B. cast iron pipe nipples
    C. flanged pipe fittings         D. threaded cast iron reducing tees

24. If a 110 volt lamp were used on a 220 volt circuit, the
    A. fuse would burn out           B. lamp would burn out
    C. line would overheat           D. lamp would flicker

25. The third prong on the plug of portable electric power tools of recent manufacture is for
    A. using the tool on a 3-phase power outlet
    B. eliminating interference in radio or television sets
    C. grounding the tool as a safety precaution
    D. using the tool on direct current circuits

26. When changing brushes on a scrubbing machine, of the following, the FIRST step to take is to
    A. lock the switch in the *off* position
    B. be sure the power cable electric plug supplying the machine is disconnected from the wall outlet
    C. place the machine on top of the positioned brushes
    D. dip the brushes in water

27. In cleaning away branches that have been broken off as a result of a severe storm, one of your men comes in contact with a live electric line and falls unconscious.
    After having removed him from contact, the FIRST thing to be done is to
    A. send for an inhalator to revive him
    B. administer mouth-to-mouth resuscitation
    C. search for the switch to prevent any other such cases
    D. loosen his clothing and begin rubbing his forehead to restore circulation

28. Of the following, the MOST effective way to reduce waste in cleaning equipment and tools is by
    A. requiring a worn brush or broom to be returned before issuing a new one
    B. requiring the cleaners to use all cleaning tools for specific periods of time
    C. keeping careful records of how frequently cleaning equipment and tools are issued to cleaners
    D. making sure that cleaners use the tools properly

29. A window cleaner should carefully examine his safety belt
    A. once a week
    B. before he puts it on each time
    C. once a month
    D. once before he enters a building

30. One of your cleaners was injured as a result of slipping on an oily floor.
    This type of accident is MOST likely due to
    A. defective equipment
    B. the physical condition of the cleaner
    C. failure to use proper safety appliances
    D. poor housekeeping

31. One important use of accident reports is to provide information that may be used to reduce the possibility of similar accidents.
    The MOST valuable entry on the report for this purpose is the
    A. name of the victim
    B. injury sustained by the victim
    C. cause of the accident
    D. location of the accident

32. Fires in buildings are of such complexity that
    A. no plans or methods of attack can be formulated in advance
    B. no planned procedures can be relied on
    C. an appointed committee is necessary to direct fighting at the fire
    D. the problem must be considered in advance and methods of attack formulated

33. Of the following types of fires, a soda-acid fire extinguisher is NOT recommended for
    A. electric motor controls
    B. waste paper
    C. waste rags
    D. wood desks

34. A foam-type fire extinguisher extinguishes fires by
    A. cooling only
    B. drenching only
    C. smothering only
    D. cooling and smothering

35. If a keg of nails had on it the words *Net Weight 10 pounds*, it would mean that the
    A. keg weighed 10 pounds without the nails
    B. nails and the keg together weighed 10 pounds
    C. nails weighed 10 pounds without the keg
    D. weight of 10 pounds is approximate

36. In deciding which items should be stored together, the one of the following factors which is usually of LEAST importance is
    A. activity     B. class     C. cost     D. size

37. Of the following, the MOST effective way to teach a subordinate how to store an item is to
    A. do it yourself while explaining
    B. explain the procedure verbally
    C. have him do it while you criticize
    D. let him look at photographs of the operation

38. If a cleaner is doing excellent work, then the PROPER action of the custodian is to
    A. give him preferential assignments as a reward
    B. tell the other cleaners what excellent work he is doing
    C. praise his work at the earlies opportunity
    D. do nothing since the man may become over-confident

39. A cleaner does very good work, but he has trouble getting to work on time. To get the man to come on time, you should
    A. bring him up on charges to stop the lateness once and for all
    B. have him report directly to you every time he is late
    C. talk over the problem with him to find its cause and possible solution
    D. threaten to transfer him if he cannot get to work on time

40. When the National flag is to be flown at half staff, it should ALWAYS be hoisted
    A. slowly to half staff
    B. slowly to the peak of staff and then lowered slowly to half staff
    C. briskly to the peak of staff and then lowered slowly to half staff
    D. briskly to the peak of staff and then lowered briskly to half staff

## KEY (CORRECT ANSWERS)

| | | | | | | | |
|---|---|---|---|---|---|---|---|
| 1. | B | 11. | C | 21. | A | 31. | C |
| 2. | D | 12. | A | 22. | C | 32. | D |
| 3. | B | 13. | B | 23. | C | 33. | A |
| 4. | D | 14. | B | 24. | B | 34. | D |
| 5. | B | 15. | B | 25. | C | 35. | C |
| 6. | A | 16. |   | 26. | B | 36. | C |
| 7. | A | 17. | C | 27. | B | 37. | A |
| 8. | A | 18. | C | 28. | D | 38. | C |
| 9. | B | 19. | C | 29. | B | 39. | C |
| 10. | D | 20. | D | 30. | D | 40. | C |

# EXAMINATION SECTION
## TEST 1

DIRECTIONS: Each question or incomplete statement is followed by several suggested answers or completions. Select the one that BEST answers the question or completes the statement. *PRINT THE LETTER OF THE CORRECT ANSWER IN THE SPACE AT THE RIGHT.*

1. In city schools, wiring for motors or lighting is
   A. 208-220 volt, 4 wire, 60 cycle
   B. 240-110 volt, 3 wire, 4 phase
   C. 120-208 volt, 3 phase, 4 wire
   D. 160-210 volt, 4 phase, 3 wire

2. The LEAST likely cause of continuous vibration in a motor-driven pump is
   A. misalignment of motor and pump
   B. loose bearings in motor
   C. poor electric connection
   D. lack of graphite lubrication

3. A starter for fluorescent lights should be ordered in
   A. volts
   B. amps
   C. current
   D. watts

4. A pipe is 50' long. If it drops ¼" each foot, how many inches does it drop in 50'?
   A. 5.5
   B. 8
   C. 10
   D. 12.5

5. A plumber's friend operates by
   A. oscillation of water and air in the pipe
   B. density of water and pressure
   C. snake action
   D. water pressure only

6. Compound is applied to pipe thread.
   When threading pipe, where would you apply compound?
   A. Male and female thread
   B. Female only
   C. Male only
   D. At the end of the male connection only

7. A 6/32 thread refers to
   A. stove bolt
   B. pipe thread
   C. machine thread
   D. drill bit

8. To hang a bulletin board on plaster or hollow tile wall, use
   A. self-tapping screws
   B. wire cut nails
   C. expansion shields
   D. molly shank and screw

9. To relieve the vacuum on a pump, one of the following should operate:
   A. discharge valve
   B. vacuum breaker
   C. foot valve
   D. bleeder valve

10. When water in circulating line shows brown, the LIKELY cause is
    A. bacteria build-up
    B. rust
    C. sluggish circulation
    D. water treatment plan excessive chemical build-up

11. The purpose of rear chamber in an incinerator is for
    A. arresting sparks            B. removing noxious gases
    C. smoke reduction             D. an extra source of $O_2$

12. A stack switch will shut down an oil burner when
    A. the temperature of the oil is low    B. steam pressure is too high
    C. there is flame failure               D. oil pressure is low

13. A check valve in a low pressure boiler water line is to
    A. prevent contamination of boiler water
    B. prevent return flow of water
    C. equalize boiler water level
    D. prevent the pressure from increasing

14. A custodian should know
    A. how to repair equipment     B. condition before breakdown
    C. right lubrication to use    D. outside conditions

15. In removing grass stains from marble and wood, which of the following should be used?
    A. Oxalic acid                 B. Muriatic acid
    C. Sodium silicate             D. Disodium silicate

16. If concrete cracks appear in spring and winter, the cause is MOST likely
    A. poor concrete mix
    B. too much foot traffic
    C. poor sub-soil drainage
    D. not enough room for expansion and contraction

17. Venetian blinds should be cleaned by
    A. using feather duster        B. vacuuming
    C. washing with clear water    D. washing with cleaning solution

18. To keep chrome-plated metal clean, you should
    A. polish with fine steel wool
    B. wash with soapy water and polish with soft cloth
    C. clean with scouring powder and polish with soft cloth
    D. none of the above

19. After wetting down the floor with water solution, the BEST mop to use is
    A. a mop wet with clean water      B. one wrung out in solution water
    C. a dry mop                       D. one wrung out in clear water

20. After sweeping and dusting a room, the LAST thing that should be done is
    A. empty waste basket
    B. switch off lights
    C. close windows
    D. clean the furniture

21. A preheater is used to heat #_____ oil.
    A. 1    B. 2    C. 4    D. 6

22. If paint blisters on the wall, the MOST likely cause is
    A. too much paint
    B. porous plaster
    C. moisture in wall
    D. hair-line plaster cracks

23. Cracks in newly plastered walls should be filled with
    A. putty
    B. rough plaster first
    C. spackling plaster
    D. silicone gel-fill

24. The BEST reason for cleaning lightbulbs is
    A. the bulb will last longer
    B. removing dust
    C. obtaining optimum light
    D. preventing electric shock

25. The color of fire lines is
    A. yellow    B. green    C. brown    D. red

26. To neutralize acid soil, which of the following should be used?
    A. Nitrogen    B. Potash    C. Phosphorus    D. Lime

27. A cleaning detergent is composed of
    A. cleaning acids
    B. salts
    C. sodium compounds
    D. alkaline compounds

28. The BEST method to use in watering trees and shrubs is to use
    A. jet-type velocity at roots
    B. hose with fine nozzle spray once a week and done well
    C. a hose only when needed to soak roots
    D. rotating single jet sprinkler

29. As a custodian, which of the following instructions would you give your staff in case of fire?
    A. Report to principal
    B. Go to location and put out fire
    C. Pull nearest fire alarm station box
    D. Make sure each one knows in advance their assigned location of duty when alarm rings

30. Which of the following effects does a foam extinguisher have?
    A. Smothering
    B. Cooling and smothering
    C. Wetting down
    D. Insulating

31. The BEST fire extinguisher to use on electric motors is
    A. soda-acid
    B. foam type
    C. carbon dioxide
    D. water

32. Two employees are arguing about their personal clothing locker. How would you handle this dispute?
    A. Reprimand both men
    B. Talk to them individually
    C. Speak to both of them together about it
    D. Write up a disciplinary report on both men

33. A fertilizer 5-10-5 means
    A. 5 potash – 10 nitrogen – phosphorous
    B. 5 tobacco chip – 10 potash – 5 phosphoric acid
    C. 5 tobacco chip – 10 nitrogen – 5 potash
    D. 5 potassium – 10 nitrogen – 5 phosphorous

34. Sand gravel mix should be
    A. 1 sand, 2 gravel, 3 cement
    B. 1 cement, 2 gravel, 3 sand
    C. 1 cement, 2 sand, 3 gravel
    D. 2 cement, 3 sand, 2 gravel

35. _____ is found between the boiler and boiler safety valve.
    A. Check valve
    B. No valve
    C. Steam stop valve
    D. Regulating valve

# KEY (CORRECT ANSWERS)

| | | | |
|---|---|---|---|
| 1. B | 11. C | 21. D | 31. C |
| 2. C | 12. C | 22. C | 32. B |
| 3. D | 13. A | 23. B | 33. A |
| 4. D | 14. B | 24. C | 34. C |
| 5. A | 15. A | 25. D | 35. B |
| 6. C | 16. D | 26. D | |
| 7. C | 17. A | 27. C | |
| 8. C | 18. B | 28. C | |
| 9. B | 19. C | 29. D | |
| 10. C | 20. B | 30. B | |

# TEST 2

DIRECTIONS: Each question or incomplete statement is followed by several suggested answers or completions. Select the one that BEST answers the question or completes the statement. *PRINT THE LETTER OF THE CORRECT ANSWER IN THE SPACE AT THE RIGHT.*

1. Of the following, the BEST procedure in sweeping classroom floors is:  1.____
    A. Open all windows before beginning the sweeping operation
    B. The cleaner should move forward while sweeping
    C. Alternate pull and push strokes should be used
    D. Sweep under desks on both sides of an aisle while moving down the aisle

2. Proper care of floor brushes includes  2.____
    A. washing brushes daily after each use with warm soap solution
    B. dipping brushes in kerosene periodically to remove dirt
    C. washing with warm soap solution at least once a month
    D. avoiding contact with soap or soda solutions to prevent drying of bristles

3. An ADVANTAGE of vacuum cleaning rather than sweeping a floor with a floor brush is that  3.____
    A. stationary furniture will not be touched by the cleaning tool
    B. the problem of dust on furniture is reduced
    C. the initial cost of the apparatus is less than the cost of an equivalent number of floor brushes
    D. daily sweeping of rooms and corridors can be eliminated

4. Sweeping compound for use on rubber tile, asphalt tile, or sealed wood floors must NOT contain  4.____
    A. sawdust    B. water    C. oil soap    D. floor oil

5. Of the following, the MOST desirable material to use in dusting furniture is a  5.____
    A. soft cotton cloth        B. hand towel
    C. counter brush            D. feather duster

6. In high dusting of walls and ceiling, the CORRECT procedure is to  6.____
    A. begin with the lower walls and proceed up to the ceiling
    B. remove pictures and window shades only if they are dusty
    C. clean the windows thoroughly before dusting any other part of the room
    D. begin with the ceiling and then dust the walls

7. When cleaning a classroom, the cleaner should  7.____
    A. dust desks before sweeping
    B. dust desks after sweeping
    C. open windows wide during the desk dusting process
    D. begin dusting at rows most distant from entrance door

8. Too much water on asphalt tile is objectionable MAINLY because the tile
   A. will tend to become discolored or spotted
   B. may be loosened from the floor
   C. tends to disintegrate prematurely
   D. becomes too slippery to walk on

9. To reduce the slip hazard resulting from waxing linoleum, the MOST practical of the following methods is to
   A. apply the wax in one heavy coat
   B. apply the wax after varnishing the linoleum
   C. buff the wax surface thoroughly
   D. apply the wax in several thin coats

10. Assume that the water-emulsion wax needed for routine waxing in your building is 15 gallons per month. This wax is supplied in 55 gallon drums.
    To cover your needs for a year, the MINIMUM number of drums you should have to request is
    A. two     B. three     C. four     D. six

11. In washing down walls, the correct procedure is to start at the bottom of the wall and work to the top.
    The MOST important reason for this is
    A. dirt streaking will tend to be avoided or easily removed
    B. less cleansing agent will be required
    C. rinse water will not be required
    D. the time for cleaning the wall is less than if washing started at the top of the wall

12. In mopping a wood floor of a classroom, the cleaner should
    A. mop against the grain of the wood wherever possible
    B. mop as large an area as possible at one time
    C. wet the floor before mopping with a cleaning agent
    D. mop only aisles and clear areas and use a scrub brush under desks and chairs

13. A precaution to observe in mopping asphalt tile floors is:
    A. Keep all pails off such floors because they will leave water marks
    B. Do not wear rubber footwear while mopping these floors
    C. Use circular motion in rinsing and drying the floor to avoid streaking
    D. Never use a cleaning agent containing trisodium phosphate

14. The MOST commonly used cleansing agent for the removal of ink stains from a wood floor is
    A. kerosene           B. oxalic acid
    C. lye                D. bicarbonate of soda

15. The FIRST operation in routine cleaning of toilets and washrooms is to
    A. wash floors        B. clean walls
    C. clean wash basins  D. empty waste receptacles

16. To eliminate the cause of odors in toilet rooms, the tile floors should be mopped with  16.____
    A. a mild solution of soap and trisodium phosphate in water
    B. dilute lye solution followed by a hot water rinse
    C. dilute muriatic acid dissolved in hot water
    D. carbon tetrachloride dissolved in hot water

17. The principal reason why soap should NOT be used in cleaning windows is that  17.____
    A. it causes loosening of the putty
    B. it may cause rotting of the wood frame
    C. a film is left on the window, requiring additional rinsing
    D. frequent use of soap will cause the glass to become permanently clouded

18. The CHIEF value of having windows consisting of many small panes of glass is  18.____
    A. the window is much stronger
    B. accident hazards are eliminated
    C. cost of replacing broken panes is low
    D. cleaning windows consisting of small panes is easier than cleaning a window with a large undivided pane

19. Cleansing powders such as Ajax should not be used to clean and polish brass MAINLY because  19.____
    A. the brass turns a much darker color
    B. such cleansers have no effect on tarnish
    C. the surface of the brass may become scratched
    D. too much fine dust is raised in the polishing process

20. To remove chalk marks on sidewalks and cemented playground areas, the MOST acceptable cleaning method is  20.____
    A. using a brush with warm water
    B. using a brush with warm water containing some kerosene
    C. hosing down such areas with water
    D. using a brush with a solution of muriatic acid in water

21. The MOST important reason for oiling wood floors is that  21.____
    A. it keeps the dust from rising during the sweeping process
    B. the need for daily sweeping of classroom floors is eliminated
    C. oiled floors present a better appearance than waxed floors
    D. the wood surface will become waterproof and stain-proof

22. After oil has been sprayed on a wood floor, the sprayer should be cleaned before storing it.  22.____
    The usual cleaning material for this purpose is
    A. ammonia water      B. salt
    C. kerosene           D. alcohol

23. The MOST desirable agent for routine cleaning of slate blackboards is
    A. warm water containing trisodium phosphate
    B. mild soap solution in warm water
    C. kerosene in warm water
    D. warm water alone

24. Neatsfoot oil is commonly used to
    A. oil light machinery
    B. prepare sweeping compound
    C. clean metal fixtures
    D. treat leather-covered chairs

25. Of the following daily jobs in the schedule of a custodian, the one he should do FIRST in the morning is to
    A. hang out the flag
    B. open all doors of the school
    C. fire boilers
    D. dust the principal's office

26. When a school custodian is newly assigned to a building at the start of the school term, his FIRST step should be to
    A. examine the building to determine needed maintenance and repair
    B. meet the principal and discuss plans for operation and maintenance of the building
    C. call a meeting of the teaching and custodial staff to explain his plans for the building
    D. review the records of maintenance and operation left by the previous custodian

27. A detergent is a material used GENERALLY for
    A. coating floors to resist water
    B. snow removal
    C. insulation of steam and hot water lines
    D. cleaning purposes

28. A good disinfectant is one that will
    A. have a clean odor which will cover up disagreeable odors
    B. destroy germs and create more sanitary conditions
    C. dissolve encrusted dirt and other sources of disagreeable odors
    D. dissolve grease and other materials that may cause stoppages in toilet waste lines

29. To help prevent leaks at the joints of water lines, the pipe threads are commonly covered with
    A. tar
    B. cup grease
    C. rubber cement
    D. white lead

30. The advantage of using screws instead of nails is that
    A. they have greater holding power
    B. they are available in a greater variety than are nails
    C. a hammer is not required for joining wood members
    D. they are less expensive

31. Of the following, the grade of steel wool that is the FINEST is  31.____
    A. 00	B. 0	C. 1	D. 2

32. The material used with solder to make it stick better is  32.____
    A. oakum	B. lye	C. oil	D. flux

33. In using a floor brush in a corridor, a cleaner should be instructed to  33.____
    A. use moderately long pull strokes whenever possible
    B. make certain that there is no overlap on sweeping strokes
    C. give the brush a slight jerk after each stroke to free it of loose dirt
    D. keep the sweeping surface of the brush firmly flat on the floor to obtain maximum coverage

34. A device installed in a drainage system to prevent gases from flowing into a building is called a  34.____
    A. trap	B. stall	C. cleanout	D. bidet

35. The plumbing fixture that contains a ball cock is the  35.____
    A. trap	B. water closet
    C. sprinkler	D. dishwasher

## KEY (CORRECT ANSWERS)

| | | | |
|---|---|---|---|
| 1. B | 11. A | 21. A | 31. A |
| 2. C | 12. C | 22. C | 32. D |
| 3. B | 13. A | 23. D | 33. C |
| 4. D | 14. B | 24. D | 34. A |
| 5. A | 15. D | 25. C | 35. B |
| 6. D | 16. A | 26. B | |
| 7. B | 17. C | 27. D | |
| 8. B | 18. C | 28. B | |
| 9. D | 19. C | 29. D | |
| 10. C | 20. A | 30. A | |

# EXAMINATION SECTION
## TEST 1

DIRECTIONS: Each question or incomplete statement is followed by several suggested answers or completions. Select the one that BEST answers the question or completes the statement. *PRINT THE LETTER OF THE CORRECT ANSWER IN THE SPACE AT THE RIGHT.*

1. The safety device on an elevator door is called the  1.____
   A. governor   B. gate-switch   C. interlock   D. safety fuse

2. Which of the following is the PROPER method of cleaning a room?  2.____
   A. Dust, empty wastebasket, sweep
   B. Empty wastebasket, dust, sweep
   C. Empty wastebasket, sweep, dust
   D. Sweep, dust, empty wastebasket

3. How would you determine when a waxed floor should be stripped?  3.____
   When
   A. someone slipped on the floor
   B. wax builds up
   C. scuffs are not removed by buffing
   D. someone complains

4. To remove modeling plaster from the floor, you should use  4.____
   A. a sharp chisel         B. a putty knife
   C. a floor-scrubbing machine   D. sulphuric acid

5. Which of the following floors would you NOT seal?  5.____
   A. Terrazzo   B. Cork   C. Asphalt   D. Tile

6. A mixing valve for domestic water blends  6.____
   A. cold water with hot boiler water
   B. hot and cold water
   C. cold water and hot water from coil submerged in boiler water
   D. hot and cold water from cooling coil

7. For sweeping under the radiators, the BEST tool to use is a  7.____
   A. dry mop          B. feather duster
   C. counter brush    D. floor broom

8. A wet return line is  8.____
   A. one containing air and water   B. above boiler water level
   C. below boiler water level       D. a condenser oil

65

9. A dry return line is
    A. one containing air only
    B. above boiler water level
    C. one containing air and water
    D. a line with a bleeder valve

10. The purpose of a fusetron is to
    A. provide motor starting current
    B. keep motor at rated speed
    C. protect from overload
    D. maintain constant motor speed

11. If combination faucet is in off position and water leaks from swivel, you should
    A. replace faucet washers
    B. repack swivel gland
    C. replace both washers and tighten swivel gland
    D. replace the faucet

12. The MAIN purpose of peat moss use is to
    A. improve soil condition
    B. fertilize soil
    C. help to keep soil moist
    D. retard the growth of weeds

13. Which of the following valves does NOT have a wheel and stem?
    A. Globe    B. Gate    C. Check    D. Plug cock

14. If a radiator is air-bound, the MOST likely cause is
    A. no condensate return
    B. defective steam valve
    C. defective air valve
    D. too much air carried in steam

15. The MAIN purpose of keeping accident reports on file is to
    A. have a record to show a lawyer
    B. contain cause of accident
    C. inform principal of how it happened
    D. provide full information for official use

16. To repair a continually flushing flushometer, you should
    A. cut down on supply valve
    B. shut off water
    C. clean out flushometer
    D. replace defective parts

17. When a repair is required, the LEAST likely thing to be done is:
    A. Determine if your staff can handle it
    B. Find out just what has to be done
    C. Ask for assistance from repair shops
    D. Decide which tools are needed to do the job

18. At which of the following locations should you find a remote control switch?
    A. In principal's office
    B. In engineer's office
    C. At boiler room entrance
    D. At entrance to building

19. Sprinkler systems are more often found in the following location:
    A. Boiler room
    B. Gym
    C. Storage rooms
    D. Science rooms

20. If a gas range flame is all whitish yellow, what does it indicate?
    A. Insufficient gas pressure  B. Insufficient air
    C. Not enough gas  D. Too much air

21. If glass on water column breaks when boiler is operating, you should
    A. bank fire  B. shut off burner
    C. use tri-cocks  D. close main steam valve

22. The BEST reason for setting a time limit on the job is
    A. time available
    B. if completion is urgent
    C. if maximum output is affected this way
    D. the men are more likely to complete the job on time

23. The safety device on a gas line is called
    A. gas cock  B. automatic pilot
    C. solenoid valve  D. safety shut-off valve

24. The MOST efficient boiler fuel operation is
    A. low $CO_2$ high CO, low stack gas temperature
    B. high $CO_2$ low CO, low stack gas temperature
    C. high firebox temperature, high $CO_2$ high stack temperature
    D. high $CO_2$ low CO, high stack gas temperature

25. The central vacuum cleaning system should be cleaned
    A. weekly  B. twice weekly
    C. daily  D. when necessary

26. If you had too much oil, what would you do for good combustion?
    A. Increase secondary air  B. Increase primary air
    C. Increase both  D. Lower oil pressure

27. The purpose of blowing down the water column is to
    A. make sure there is enough water
    B. keep the gauge glass clean
    C. determine the true water level
    D. make sure you have steam in boiler

28. Water hammer in water lines is caused by
    A. velocity of air and water
    B. defective faucet
    C. defective washers
    D. quick opening and closing of faucets

29. The CHIEF reason for a plumbing system trap is to
    A. equalize waste  B. provide good drainage
    C. provide water seal  D. none of the above

30. A vapor barrier is used for
    A. insulating electrically
    B. protecting against low temperature
    C. a moisture barrier
    D. exterior condensation on cold water pipes

31. The material recommended for removing blood or fruit stains from concrete is
    A. soft soap    B. neatsfoot oil    C. oxalic acid    D. ammonia

32. For what purpose are panic bars used? To
    A. make sure door is locked          B. provide easy exit
    C. meet fire department regulations  D. keep door open

33. To detect a leak in the gas line, which of the following would you do?
    A. Call gas company       B. Use a soapy solution
    C. Use a lighted match    D. Smell the area

34. To preserve freshly laid concrete, you would
    A. cover it                         B. keep it moist
    C. keep it at a temperature of 60°F C. keep it at a temperature over 60°F

35. Gas is measured in
    A. thousands cubic feet           B. hundreds cubic feet
    C. ten thousands cubic feet volume D. 100,000 cubic feet volume

36. The FIRST thing a window cleaner should do is
    A. test window bolts      B. see that cleaning tools are good
    C. check window belt      D. not lean too heavily on glass

37. Couplings on gas supply line serve the same purpose as
    A. electrical conduit    B. machine threads
    C. right and left hand   D. water unions

38. Before a custodian leaves the building, he would be LEAST likely to
    A. lower the flag        B. remove hazards
    C. tidy the stock room   D. check all entry doors

39. Which of the following would you NOT use to paint chain-link fences?
    A. Brush        B. Sprayer
    C. Roller       D. None of the above

40. Which of the following steps should be taken in closing a low pressure boiler at the end of heating season in preparation for lay-up?
    A. Empty water, close valves, drop fire
    B. Dump fire, close valves, let boiler cool, empty water
    C. Dump fire, let boiler cool, empty water, close valves
    D. None of the above

## KEY (CORRECT ANSWERS)

| | | | | | | | |
|---|---|---|---|---|---|---|---|
| 1. | C | 11. | A | 21. | C | 31. | D |
| 2. | C | 12. | C | 22. | D | 32. | B |
| 3. | B | 13. | C | 23. | C | 33. | B |
| 4. | B | 14. | C | 24. | B | 34. | B |
| 5. | C | 15. | D | 25. | B | 35. | A |
| 6. | B | 16. | D | 26. | B | 36. | C |
| 7. | C | 17. | C | 27. | C | 37. | C |
| 8. | C | 18. | C | 28. | A | 38. | C |
| 9. | B | 19. | C | 29. | C | 39. | B |
| 10. | C | 20. | D | 30. | C | 40. | B |

# TEST 2

DIRECTIONS: Each question or incomplete statement is followed by several suggested answers or completions. Select the one that BEST answers the question or completes the statement. *PRINT THE LETTER OF THE CORRECT ANSWER IN THE SPACE AT THE RIGHT.*

1. The lowest visible part of the water column attached to an HRT boiler should be AT LEAST
   A. 3 inches above the top row of tubes
   B. 6 inches above the fusible plug
   C. 1 inch above the top row of tubes
   D. ½ inch above the fusible plug

   1.____

2. The function of a fusible plug is to
   A. melt if the water temperature is too high
   B. prevent too high a furnace temperature
   C. prevent excessive steam pressure from developing in the boiler
   D. melt when the water level drops below the level of the plug

   2.____

3. To control the temperature of water in a domestic water supply tank, the device used is USUALLY a
   A. thermostat          B. pressuretrol
   C. solenoid valve      D. aquastat

   3.____

4. A house trap is a device placed in the house drain immediately inside the foundation wall of the building.
   Its MAIN purpose is to
   A. trap sediment flowing in the house drain to the street sewer
   B. prevent sewer gases from circulating in the building plumbing system
   C. maintain air pressure balance in the vent lines of the plumbing system
   D. provide a means for cleaning the waste lines of the plumbing system

   4.____

5. In the care and operation of steam boilers, a procedure that is considered GOOD practice is to
   A. open the safety valve in the event low water is found
   B. refill the boiler with cold water when the boiler is hot
   C. remove the boiler from service immediately if the water level cannot be determined because the gauge glass is broken
   D. use hot water where possible in refilling a boiler prior to firing

   5.____

6. The addition of moisture to coal to promote combustion of coal is commonly referred to as
   A. tempering    B. dusting    C. watering    D. dehumidifying

   6.____

7. The purpose of fire doors in a building is to
   A. prevent fires           B. prevent arson
   C. avoid panic             D. prevent the spread of fire

   7.____

8. Of the following, the type of fire extinguisher that is MOST satisfactory for use on a fire in a place of operating electrical equipment is
   A. carbon dioxide
   B. sand pail
   C. soda acid
   D. foam

9. The device which is LEAST likely to be used by the custodian in cleaning minor stoppages in the plumbing system is a
   A. snake   B. auger   C. plunger   D. trowel

10. The PROPER cleaning agent for a paint brush that has been used to shellac a floor is
    A. gasoline   B. linseed oil   C. alcohol   D. turpentine

11. In cutting the ends of a number of lengths of wood at an angle of 45°, one would PREFERABLY use a
    A. protractor
    B. triangle
    C. miter box
    D. movable head T-square

12. To the custodian, the term *zeolite* refers to
    A. boiler insulation
    B. combustion chamber refractories
    C. boiler tube cleaning agent
    D. boiler water softening

13. A custodian notices a man in a corridor of the building. This visitor identifies himself as a police officer and states that he is observing a student in one of the classes.
    The custodian
    A. make no further inquiry of the police officer
    B. ask the police officer to check with the school principal if he has not already done so
    C. ask for all details, the name of the student, and reason for observation so that he can report the visit in his log book
    D. ask the police officer to leave the building unless he has received permission from the Board of Education in writing

14. When a paint coat blisters, the cause is USUALLY:
    A. Paint coat is too thick
    B. Plaster pores not sealed properly
    C. Moisture under the paint coat
    D. Too much oil in paint

15. Galvanized iron pails resist rusting because the surface of the iron is coated with
    A. copper   B. zinc   C. aluminum   D. lead

16. To maintain brick walls and to eliminate or prevent leaks, the walls are USUALLY
    A. painted   B. sprayed   C. pointed   D. refaced

17. A safety device that can be used instead of a fuse to protect a piece of electrical equipment is a
    A. circuit breaker
    B. rheostat
    C. toggle switch
    D. relay

18. Custodians are required to abide by snow removal regulations, which state that snow be removed
    A. from sidewalks within four hours after snow ceases to fall during daytime
    B. from sidewalks within 24 hours after snowfall ceases
    C. within a reasonable period only from walks immediately in front of school entrances
    D. from sidewalks within 12 hours only if the fall is greater than four inches

19. Which of the following types of grates should be used for ease in cleaning fires when hand firing large boilers under natural draft at heavy loads with #1 buckwheat?
    A. Dumping grates
    B. Stationary grates with ¾" air spaces
    C. Stationary grates (pinhole type)
    D. Shaking grates

20. Which of the following fuels contains the GREATEST number of heat units per pound?
    A. Hard coal
    B. #6 fuel oil
    C. Yard screenings
    D. Bituminous coal

21. The purpose of admitting air over the fire in a coal-fired furnace is USUALLY to
    A. reduce the stack gases temperature
    B. improve the draft
    C. reduce the smoke
    D. reduce the draft

22. In most usual types of large capacity oil burners using #6 oil, under fully automatic control, the atomization of the oil is produced by the
    A. pressure from the pump
    B. pressure from the secondary air fan
    C. oil temperature from the heater
    D. rotation of the burner assembly by the motor

23. Which of the following comes the closest to indicating the number of degree-days in a normal heating season in New York City?
    A. 3000   B. 4000   C. 5000   D. 6000

24. A badly sooted HRT boiler under coal firing will show a _____ than a clean boiler.
    A. higher $CO_2$ value
    B. lower $CO_2$ value
    C. higher stack temperature
    D. lower draft loss

25. The direct room radiator in a school with a pneumatically controlled steam heating system is cold, while the adjoining rooms are heated adequately.
Of the following, the FIRST thing you would check in the room is the
    A. steam pipe in the room before the pneumatic steam valve
    B. thermostat
    C. pneumatic steam valve
    D. thermostatic trap

26. A vaporstat used on a fully automatic heavy oil burning rotary cup installation, with separate motor driven oil pump, is GENERALLY used to
    A. keep the boiler pressure within proper limits
    B. regulate the pressure of the primary air
    C. regulate the pressure of the secondary air
    D. shut down the burner when primary air failure occurs

27. Suppose that a small oil fire has broken out in the boiler room of your building.
Of the following, the one that is LEAST suitable as an extinguisher is
    A. soda acid            B. pyrene (carbon tetra chloride
    C. foamite              D. carbon dioxide

28. An electric elevator car stalls on the ground floor of a school building.
Of the following, the item you would be LEAST likely to check in your inspection is
    A. *baby switch*        B. floor door switch
    C. limit switch         D. current to elevator motors

29. In an investigation of a complaint of sewer gas from a urinal in a regularly used toilet room, you find that the trap seal has been lost.
The LEAST common cause of this condition is
    A. evaporation of water from the trap
    B. vent blocked up
    C. high wind over roof vent
    D. self-siphonage

30. Of the following, the cleaning assignment which you would LEAST prefer to have performed during school hours is
    A. sweeping of corridors and stairs
    B. cleaning and polishing brass fixtures
    C. cleaning toilets
    D. dusting of offices, halls, and special rooms

31. BEST combustion conditions exist when the stack haze as indicated on the Ringelman chart scale is Number
    A. 1            B. 3            C. 5            D. 6

32. A pop safety valve is commonly a
    A. member with a rupture section    B. dead weight valve
    C. ball and lever valve              D. spring-loaded valve

33. Fusible plugs used as protective devices in HRT boilers producing low pressure steam should melt at temperatures
    A. above the temperature of the steam and below the temperature of the flue gases
    B. at the same temperature as the steam
    C. above the usual temperature of both the flue gases and the steam
    D. at about the same temperature as the flue gases

34. The high low water alarm of a steam boiler is USUALLY located in the
    A. boiler           B. gauge glass
    C. water column     D. feedwater

35. What is an advantage of shaking grates over stationary grates?
    A. The fire can be cleaned without opening the fire door.
    B. They are warp-proof.
    C. They are usually more sturdily constructed than stationary grates.
    D. Deeper firebed can usually be maintained.

36. An ACCEPTABLE method of detecting air leaks in the setting of a boiler is
    A. placing an open flame or burning torch near the point where the leaks are suspected
    B. coating the suspected parts of the setting with heavy grease
    C. coating the suspected points of leakage with a heavy soap emulsion
    D. inspecting suspected areas of leakage with a powerful light and hand magnifier

37. In a plumbing installation, an escutcheon is a
    A. metal collar     B. reducing tee
    C. valve            D. single sweep

38. A leaking faucet system can be repaired by replacing the
    A. flange or the seat       B. nipple
    C. o-ring or the packing    D. cock

39. The abbreviation O.S. and Y, as used in plumbing, apply to a(n)
    A. hot well    B. radiator    C. injector    D. gate valve

40. Gas range piping should have a MINIMUM diameter of _____ inch.
    A. ¾    B. ½    C. ¼    D. ⅛

## KEY (CORRECT ANSWERS)

| | | | |
|---|---|---|---|
| 1. A | 11. C | 21. C | 31. A |
| 2. D | 12. D | 22. D | 32. D |
| 3. D | 13. B | 23. C | 33. B |
| 4. B | 14. C | 24. C | 34. C |
| 5. C | 15. B | 25. A | 35. A |
| 6. A | 16. C | 26. D | 36. A |
| 7. D | 17. A | 27. A | 37. A |
| 8. A | 18. A | 28. C | 38. C |
| 9. D | 19. A | 29. A | 39. D |
| 10. C | 20. B | 30. D | 40. A |

# EXAMINATION SECTION
## TEST 1

DIRECTIONS: Each question or incomplete statement is followed by several suggested answers or completions. Select the one that BEST answers the question or completes the statement. *PRINT THE LETTER OF THE CORRECT ANSWER IN THE SPACE AT THE RIGHT.*

1. Of the following, the BEST practice to follow in criticizing the work performance of a cleaner is to
   A. save up several criticisms and make them all at once
   B. soften your criticisms by being humorous
   C. have another cleaner, who has more seniority, give the criticism
   D. make sure that you explain to the cleaner the reasons for your criticisms

   1.____

2. A group of students complains to you about the lack of cleanliness in the building. You realize that budget cutbacks have unavoidably led to shortages in manpower and equipment for the cleaning staff.
   Of the following, the BEST way for you to answer these students is to
   A. tell them frankly that the cleanliness of the building is none of their business
   B. apologize for the condition of the building and promise that your men will work harder
   C. tell them to take their complaints to the administration and not to you
   D. explain the reason for the building's condition and what you are doing to improve it

   2.____

3. Your supervisor has ordered you to announce to your cleaners a new cleaning rule with which you disagree.
   You should
   A. admit honestly to your cleaners that you disagree with the rule
   B. announce the rule to your cleaners without expressing your disagreement
   C. encourage your cleaners by telling them that you agree with the rule
   D. tell your supervisor that you refuse to announce any rule with which you disagree

   3.____

4. The preparation of work schedules for custodial employees and the daily work routine of these employees is determined and regulated by the
   A. principal              B. district supervisor of custodians
   C. chief of custodians    D. school custodian

   4.____

5. The records and reports of school plant operations are originated by the school custodian and forwarded on a monthly basis to the
   A. borough supervisor         B. district superintendent
   C. director of plant operations   D. chief of custodians

   5.____

6. The operation, care, maintenance, and minor repair of a school building and grounds is the duty and responsibility of the school custodian.
   This responsibility
   A. can be delegated to the custodial staff
   B. is shared with the custodial staff
   C. cannot be delegated and is the school custodian's only
   D. is shared with the district supervisor

7. A cleaner does a very good job on the work assigned to him, but on several occasions you find him lounging and reading a magazine in an isolated part of the building.
   The BEST thing for you to do is
   A. tell the man to increase the time it takes to do the job so as to reduce his lax time
   B. give him a strong reprimand
   C. check the log book or personnel records and confer with the staff and principal to see if there are any complaints against him
   D. tell the man to report to you whenever he finishes the required work

8. If one of your employees approaches you with a suggestion on how to improve work procedures, you should
   A. ignore it
   B. listen to the suggestion and take appropriate action
   C. refer the employee to the principal
   D. tell the employee to tell the union

9. When instructing a new employee, you should include all of the following EXCEPT
   A. the shortcomings, failures, and attitudes of fellow workers
   B. unusual situations and hazardous conditions of work assignments
   C. the normal hours of employment and special situations which require overtime
   D. the rules, regulations, customs, and policies of the assignment

10. You are newly assigned to a building in which the custodial staff has been working effectively for many years.
    In order to obtain the respect of the staff, you should
    A. immediately make major significant changes in procedures to establish your authority
    B. immediately make minor changes to show that you have new ideas, plans, and organizational ability
    C. criticize your predecessor to establish your identity, attitude, and authority
    D. make no changes to work schedules or assignments until you are fully aware of the existing practices, schedules or assignments

11. Suppose that a cleaner has been found to be quite negligent in his work and has been warned repeatedly by you.
    If you find that your warnings have not changed the man's attitude or work habits, the PROPER thing to do is to

A. discharge the employee
B. change his assignment in the school to a less desirable job
C. have a serious talk with the cleaner to find out why he does not do satisfactory work
D. give the cleaner a final warning

12. An after-school play center is in operation in your building. On a particular afternoon, the children in this activity are especially noisy and creating a disturbance.
    The FIRST procedure to follow is to
    A. notify the day school principal of this situation
    B. notify the teacher in charge of this situation
    C. pay no attention to this situation and forget about it
    D. notify the police

12.____

13. A school custodian is required to submit several types of written reports to his supervisor on a monthly basis. After submitting his monthly reports, a custodian discovers he has made an error.
    The CORRECT procedure for the school custodian to follow concerning this matter is to
    A. notify the supervisor and have the supervisor correct the error
    B. notify the supervisor and request the return of the report so that the custodian can correct the error
    C. take no action so that the error may be unnoticed
    D. take no action so that the supervisor may find the mistake

13.____

14. New cleaning materials are constantly appearing on the market.
    It would be ADVISABLE for the custodian engineer to
    A. sample them to determine the cost factor
    B. trial test in an operation
    C. check materials for product safety
    D. all of the above

14.____

15. All vacuum tubes in oil burner programmers, smoke detection devices, and other electronic controls should be changed
    A. as needed              B. monthly
    C. yearly                 D. every three years

15.____

16. In the event of flame failure, what occurs FIRST?
    A. Magnetic oil valve closes.      B. Metering valve reduces oil flow.
    C. Magnetic gas valve closes.      D. Primary air supply is closed.

16.____

17. A burner-mounted vaporstat is a control used in conjunction with proving
    A. ignition              B. proper oil temperature
    C. flame failure         D. primary air

17.____

18. Secondary air dampers on a boiler with a rotary cup oil burner are installed PRIMARILY to
    A. measure the flow of air into the furnace
    B. furnish air for atomization
    C. furnish air for combustion
    D. regulate boiler steam pressure

19. In a fully automatic oil burning plant, ignition of fuel oil in the firebox is accomplished by
    A. spark ignition
    B. hand torch
    C. kerosene rags
    D. spark ignition which ignites a gas pilot

20. The purpose of recirculating fuel oil is PRIMARILY to
    A. bring it up to the proper temperature
    B. heat oil in storage tanks
    C. force out air
    D. bring oil up to burner

21. The atomization of the oil in a rotary cup oil burner is PRIMARILY due to
    A. oil pressure
    B. rotary cup only
    C. secondary air
    D. rotary cup and primary air

22. A rotary cup oil burner is started and stopped by means of the
    A. magnetic oil valve
    B. modutrol motor
    C. pressuretrol
    D. vaporstat

23. The fuel oil suction strainer outside the oil storage tanks should be cleaned when
    A. burner flame fluctuates
    B. steam pressure drops
    C. flame failure occurs
    D. a differential in vacuum reading across strainer occurs

24. The LOWEST temperature at which oil gives off sufficient vapors to explode momentarily, when flame is applied, is known as _____ point.
    A. flash     B. fire     C. pour     D. atomization

25. Air/oil ratio in a rotary cup burner is correctly arrived at with the proper setting of the following:
    A. Aquastat, vaporstat, pressurestat
    B. Metering valve, primary air, pressurestat
    C. Metering valve, primary air, secondary air
    D. Aquastat, primary air, secondary air

## KEY (CORRECT ANSWERS)

| | | | | |
|---|---|---|---|---|
| 1. | D | | 11. | A |
| 2. | D | | 12. | B |
| 3. | B | | 13. | B |
| 4. | D | | 14. | D |
| 5. | A | | 15. | C |
| | | | | |
| 6. | C | | 16. | A |
| 7. | D | | 17. | D |
| 8. | B | | 18. | C |
| 9. | A | | 19. | D |
| 10. | D | | 20. | A |

| | |
|---|---|
| 21. | D |
| 22. | C |
| 23. | D |
| 24. | A |
| 25. | C |

# TEST 2

DIRECTIONS: Each question or incomplete statement is followed by several suggested answers or completions. Select the one that BEST answers the question or completes the statement. *PRINT THE LETTER OF THE CORRECT ANSWER IN THE SPACE AT THE RIGHT.*

1. The school custodian can help create goodwill and cooperation by the students, faculty, parents, visitors, and the general public through    1._____
    A. minding his own business
    B. carrying out his duties diligently
    C. reporting all infractions to the principal
    D. letting his supervisor worry about building operations

2. The school custodian has as his responsibility all of the following equipment, EXCEPT    2._____
    A. that used for educational and/or culinary purposes
    B. electrical
    C. swimming pool machinery
    D. elevator and sidewalk hoist equipment

3. Upon hiring, custodial employees are required to be    3._____
    A. x-rayed or tine tested
    B. fingerprinted and police checked
    C. issued ID cards by personnel security
    D. all of the above

4. Minor repairs consist of    4._____
    A. mechanical adjustment and repacking
    B. clearing minor stoppages and limited glazing
    C. tightening and temporary repairs
    D. all of the above

5. Plant operation of the Board of Education is a bureau within the    5._____
    A. Division of School Buildings    B. Office of Design and Construction
    C. Office of Business Affairs    D. Bureau of Maintenance

6. Of the following ways of improving the success of a safety program, the one MOST likely to secure employee acceptance and interest is    6._____
    A. frequent inspection
    B. employee participation in the program
    C. posting attractive notices in work areas and employee quarters
    D. frequent meetings of employees at which safe methods are demonstrated

7. With regard to supplies, a GOOD procedure is to utilize a daily inventory. The reason for this is that    7._____
    A. you are aware of what is on hand at all times
    B. you know if anyone is stealing
    C. it keeps you busy
    D. you can check and see if your employees are working

82

8. A school custodian notices a man in a corridor. This visitor identifies himself as a police officer and states he is observing a student in one of the classes. The school custodian should
   A. make no further inquiries
   B. ask if the police officer has checked with the school principal
   C. ask for details—the name of the student, reason for observation, etc. —so as to make a log book entry
   D. ask the officer to leave unless he has written permission from the principal

9. In filling out an accident report on an injured cleaner, the LEAST important item to include in the report is the
   A. equipment being used when the injury occurred
   B. attitude of the cleaner towards his job
   C. nature and extent of the injury
   D. work being done when the accident occurred

10. A dispute arises with a cleaner regarding his duties, where he claims the work assigned is *not his job*. After explaining his duties to him and showing him his work schedule, he still refuses to perform the disputed duties.
    To resolve this difficulty, you would
    A. fire him for insubordination
    B. notify the school principal
    C. call in the employees' union delegate
    D. call in the district supervisor of custodians

11. A number of pupil injuries have occurred while they were traveling on school stairs. Your inspection shows no defects or inadequacy of lighting.
    The MOST desirable step to take to reduce the frequency of these accidents is to
    A. assign a cleaner to each stairway when being used
    B. put up signs warning children to be careful
    C. discuss the matter with the school principal
    D. install better stair lighting and make sure handrails are in perfect order

12. The *fuel and utility* report is a record of fuel and electricity used in a school building.
    This report should be sent to the administrative supervisor
    A. daily     B. weekly     C. monthly     D. yearly

13. One of your employees is constantly dissatisfied and is always complaining. The BEST procedure to follow regarding this man is to
    A. reprimand him and warn him that his conduct is affecting the other employees and that unless he changes his attitude he will be dismissed
    B. reassign him to a job where he will be more closely supervised
    C. discuss in detail his dissatisfaction and determine the cause
    D. supervise him less closely

14. Custodial payroll reports are submitted
    A. every two weeks
    B. every four weeks
    C. monthly
    D. quarterly

15. An inventor of capital equipment must be filled out
    A. monthly
    B. upon change of custodians
    C. semi-annually
    D. yearly

16. School custodians are required to inspect their buildings for fire prevention and fire safety
    A. daily
    B. weekly
    C. monthly
    D. quarterly

17. A contractor working in your building is doing unsatisfactory repair work. You would notify, in writing, the
    A. borough or administrative supervisor
    B. district superintendent
    C. contract compliance division
    D. director of plant operations

18. If one of your employees frequently misplaces cleaning equipment, you would
    A. notify the borough supervisor
    B. handle the problem yourself
    C. call in the chief of custodians to speak to the employee
    D. tell the principal of the school and ask for action against the employee

19. Safety education of custodial employees is the direct responsibility of the
    A. school custodian
    B. principal
    C. borough supervisor
    D. director of plant operations

20. Worker's compensation insurance coverage for custodian employees is provided by all of the following EXCEPT the
    A. board of education
    B. union
    C. school custodian
    D. school

21. Request for plumbing repair which cannot be performed by the custodial staff are forwarded to the
    A. chief of custodians
    B. director of plant operations
    C. borough supervisor
    D. plumbing shops

22. The cleaning of electrical distribution panel boxes and switchboards is the responsibility of the
    A. principal
    B. school custodian
    C. district supervisor
    D. cleaner

23. A parent complains that one of your cleaner used abusive language to him. As the school custodian, you should
    A. reprimand the cleaner
    B. fire the cleaner
    C. investigate the complaint to find out if there is any basis to the allegation
    D. ignore the complaint

24. Of the following, the LARGEST individual item of custodial expense in operating a school building is generally the cost of
    A. labor
    B. fuel
    C. electricity
    D. elevator services

25. A telephone caller tells a school custodian that a bomb has been placed in the building and immediately hangs up the phone.
    The FIRST thing the school custodian should do, in the absence of the principal, is to
    A. call the fire department
    B. call the police department
    C. let the principal's subordinate handle it
    D. ignore the call since most threats are hoaxes

## KEY (CORRECT ANSWERS)

| | | | |
|---|---|---|---|
| 1. | B | 11. | C |
| 2. | A | 12. | C |
| 3. | D | 13. | C |
| 4. | D | 14. | B |
| 5. | A | 15. | D |
| 6. | B | 16. | A |
| 7. | A | 17. | A |
| 8. | B | 18. | B |
| 9. | B | 19. | A |
| 10. | A | 20. | B |

| | |
|---|---|
| 21. | C |
| 22. | B |
| 23. | C |
| 24. | A |
| 25. | B |

# EXAMINATION SECTION
# TEST 1

DIRECTIONS: Each question or incomplete statement is followed by several suggested answers or completions. Select the one that BEST answers the question or completes the statement. *PRINT THE LETTER OF THE CORRECT ANSWER IN THE SPACE AT THE RIGHT.*

1. A custodian was given a booklet that showed a new work method that could save time. He didn't tell his men because he thought that they would get the booklet anyway. For the custodian to have acted like this is a

    A. *good* idea, because he saves the time and bother of talking to the men
    B. *bad* idea, because he should make sure his men know about better work methods
    C. *good* idea, because the men would rather read about it themselves
    D. *bad* idea, because a supervisor should always show his men every memo he gets from higher authority

1.____

2. A custodian found it necessary to discipline two subordinates. One man had been operating his equipment in a wrong way, while the other man came to work late for three days in a row. The supervisor decided to talk to both men together.
For the custodian to deal with the problems in this way is a

    A. *good* idea, because each man will learn about the difficulties of the other person and how to solve such difficulties
    B. *bad* idea, because the supervisor should wait until he can bring a larger group together and save time in discussing such questions
    C. *good* idea, because he will be able to get the men to see that their problems are related
    D. *bad* idea, because he should meet with each man separately and give him his full attention

2.____

3. A custodian should try to make his men feel their jobs are important in order to

    A. get the men to say good things about their supervisor to his own superior
    B. get the men to think in terms of advancing to better jobs
    C. let higher management in the agency know that the supervisor is efficient
    D. help the men to be able to work more efficiently and enthusiastically

3.____

4. A custodian should know approximately how long it takes to do a particular kind of job CHIEFLY because he

    A. will know how much time to take if he has to do it himself
    B. will be able to tell his men to do it even faster
    C. can judge the performance of the person doing the job
    D. can retrain experienced employees in better work habits

4.____

5. Custodians often get their employees' opinions about better work methods because

    A. the men will know that they are respected
    B. the men would otherwise lose all their confidence in the supervisor
    C. the supervisor might find in this way a good suggestion he could use
    D. this is the best method for improvement of work methods

5.____

6. Right after you have trained your subordinates in doing a new job, you find that they seem to be doing all right, but that it will take them several days to finish. You also have several groups of men working at other locations. The MOST efficient way for you to make sure that the men continue doing the new job properly is to

    A. stay on that job with the men until it is finished, just in case trouble develops
    B. visit the men every half hour until the job is done
    C. stay away from their job that day, and visit the men the next day to ask them if they had any problems
    D. visit the men a few times each day until they finish the new job

7. Assume that one of your new employees is older than you are. You also think that he may be hard to get along with because he is older than you.
The BEST way for you to avoid any problems with the older worker is for you to

    A. *lay down the law* immediately and tell the man he better not cause you any trouble
    B. treat the man just the way you would any other worker
    C. always ask the older worker for advice in the presence of all the men
    D. ignore the man entirely until he realizes that you are the boss

8. Assume you have tried a new method suggested by one of your employees, and find that it is easier and cheaper than the method you had been using.
The proper thing for you to do NEXT is to

    A. say nothing to anyone, but train your men to use the new method
    B. train your men to use the new method and tell your crew that you got the idea from one of the men
    C. continue using the old method, because a supervisor should not use suggestions of his men
    D. have your crew learn the new method and take credit for the idea since you are the boss

9. Suppose you are a custodian and your superior tells you that the way your men are doing a certain procedure is wrong and that you should re-train your men as soon as possible. When you begin to re-train the men, the FIRST thing you should do is

    A. tell your men that a wrong procedure had been used and that a new method must be learned as a result
    B. train your employees in the new method with no explanation, since you are the boss
    C. tell the crew that your superior has just decided that everyone should learn a new method
    D. tell the crew that your superior says your method is wrong, but that you don't agree with this

10. It is *bad* practice to criticize a man in front of the other men because

    A. people will think you are too strict
    B. it is annoying to anyone who walks by
    C. it is embarrassing to the man concerned
    D. it will antagonize the other men

11. A custodian decides not to put his two best men on a work detail because he knows that they won't like it.
    For the custodian to make the work assignment this way is a

    A. *good* idea, because it is only fair to give your best men a break once in a while
    B. *bad* idea, because you should treat all of your men fairly and not show favoritism
    C. *good* idea, because you save the strength of these men for another job
    D. *bad* idea, because more of the men should be exempted from the assignment

12. Suppose you are a custodian and you find it inconvenient to obey an established procedure set by your agency. You think another procedure would be better.
    The BEST thing to do FIRST about this procedure that you don't like is for you to

    A. obey the procedure even if you don't want to, and suggest your idea to your own supervisor
    B. disregard the procedure because a supervisor is supposed to have some privileges
    C. follow the procedure some of the time, but ignore it when the men aren't watching
    D. organize a group of other supervisors to get the procedure changed

13. A custodian estimated that it would take his crew one workday per week to do a certain job each week. However, after a month he noticed that the job averaged two-and-a-half days a week, and this delayed other jobs that had to be done.
    The FIRST thing that the custodian should do in this case is to

    A. call his men together and warn them that they will get a poor work evaluation if they don't work harder
    B. talk to each man personally, asking him to work harder on the job
    C. go back and study the maintenance job by himself, to see if more men should be assigned to the job
    D. write his boss a report describing in detail how much time it is taking the men to do the job

14. An employee complains to you that some of his work assignments are too difficult to do alone.
    Which of the following is the BEST way for you to handle this complaint?

    A. Go with him to see exactly what he does and why he finds it so difficult.
    B. Politely tell the man that he has to do the job or be brought up on charges.
    C. Tell the man to send his complaint to the head of your agency.
    D. Sympathize with the man and give him easier jobs.

15. The BEST way for a custodian to keep control of his work assignments is to

    A. ask the men to report to him immediately when their jobs are finished
    B. walk around the buildings once a week, and get a first-hand view of what is being done
    C. keep his ears open for problems and complaints, but leave the men alone to do the work
    D. write up a work schedule, and check it periodically against the actual work done

16. A custodian made a work schedule for his men. At the bottom of it he wrote, *No changes or exceptions will be made in this schedule for any reason.*
    For the custodian to have made this statement is

    A. *good,* because the men will respect the custodian for his attitude
    B. *bad,* because there are emergencies and special situations that occur
    C. *good,* because each man will know exactly what is expected of him
    D. *bad,* because the men should expect that no changes will ever be made in the work schedule without written permission

17. Which one of the following would NOT be a result of a well-planned work schedule?
    The schedule

    A. makes efficient use of the time of the staff
    B. acts as a checklist for an important job that might be left out
    C. will give an idea of the work to a substitute supervisor
    D. shows at a glance who the best men are

18. A new piece of equipment you have ordered is delivered. You are familiar with it but the men under you, who will use it, do not know the equipment.
    Of the following methods, which is the BEST to take in explaining to them how to operate this equipment?

    A. Ask the men to watch other crews using the equipment
    B. Show one reliable man how to operate the equipment and ask him to teach the other men
    C. Ask the men to read the instructions in the manual for the equipment
    D. Call the men together and show them how to operate the equipment

19. One custodian assigns work to his men by calling his crew together each week and describing what has to be done that week. He then tells them to arrange individual assignments among themselves and to work as a team during the week.
    This method of scheduling work is a

    A. *good* idea, because this guarantees that the men will work together
    B. *bad* idea, because responsibility for doing the job is poorly fixed
    C. *good* idea, because the men will finish the job in less tirae working together
    D. *bad* idea, because the supervisor should always stay with his men

20. Suppose that a custodial assistant came to the custodian with a problem concerning his assignment.
    For the custodian to listen to this problem is a

    A. *good* idea, because a supervisor should always take time off to talk when one of his men wants to talk
    B. *bad* idea, because the supervisor should not be bothered during the work day
    C. *good* idea, because it's the job of the supervisor to deal with problems of job assignment
    D. *bad* idea, because the employee could start annoying the supervisor with all sorts of problems

21. Suppose that on the previous afternoon you were looking for an experienced employee in order to give him an emergency job and he was missing from his job location. The next morning he tells you that he got sick suddenly and had to go home, but couldn't tell you since you weren't around. He has never done this before.
    What should you do?  21.____

    A. Tell the man he is excused and that in such circumstances he did the wisest thing.
    B. Bring the man up on charges because, whatever he says, he could still have notified you.
    C. Have the man examined by a doctor to see if he really was sick the day before
    D. Explain to the man that he should make every effort to tell or to get a message to you if he must leave

22. An employee had a grievance and went to the custodian about it. The employee wasn't satisfied with the way the custodian tried to help him, and told him so. Yet the custodian had done everything he could under the circumstances.
    The PROPER action for the supervisor to take at this time is to  22.____

    A. politely tell the employee that there is nothing more for the custodian to do about the problem
    B. let the employee know how he can bring his complaint to a higher authority
    C. tell the employee that he must solve the problem on his own, since he didn't want to follow the custodian's advice
    D. suggest to the employee that he ask another supervisor for assistance

23. In which of the following situations is it BEST to give your men spoken rather than written orders?  23.____

    A. You want your men to have a record of the instructions.
    B. Spoken instructions are less likely to be forgotten.
    C. An emergency situation has arisen in which there is no time to write up instructions.
    D. There are instructions on time and leave regulations which are complicated.

24. One of your employees tells you that a week ago he had a small accident on the job, but he didn't bother telling you because he was able to continue working.
    For the employee not to have told the custodian about the accident was  24.____

    A. *good,* because the accident was a small one
    B. *bad,* because all accidents should be reported, no matter how small
    C. *good,* because the custodian should be bothered only for important matters
    D. *bad,* because having an accident is one way to get excused for the day

25. For a custodian to deal with each of his subordinates in exactly the same manner is  25.____

    A. *poor,* because each man presents a different problem and there is no other way of handling all problems
    B. *good,* because once a problem is handled with one man, he can handle another man with the same problem
    C. *poor,* because the men will resent it if they are not handled each in a better way than others
    D. *good,* because this assures fair and impartial treatment of each subordinate

6 (#1)

## KEY (CORRECT ANSWERS)

| | | | |
|---|---|---|---|
| 1. | B | 11. | B |
| 2. | D | 12. | A |
| 3. | D | 13. | C |
| 4. | C | 14. | A |
| 5. | C | 15. | D |
| 6. | D | 16. | B |
| 7. | B | 17. | D |
| 8. | B | 18. | D |
| 9. | A | 19. | B |
| 10. | C | 20. | C |

21. D
22. B
23. C
24. B
25. A

———

# TEST 2

DIRECTIONS: Each question or incomplete statement is followed by several suggested answers or completions. Select the one that BEST answers the question or completes the statement. *PRINT THE LETTER OF THE CORRECT ANSWER IN THE SPACE AT THE RIGHT.*

1. One day a custodial assistant said to the custodian, *I can get a tile cleaner that is as good as the stuff we use, and for less money, because my brother is a building contractor. How about it?*
   The CORRECT way for the custodian to handle this situation is for him to

    A. thank the assistant, but tell him that individual workers cannot buy their own cleaning material for project use
    B. tell the assistant that no one has any right to start interfering in the buying procedures of the authority
    C. go along with the assistant and buy the cleaner from his brother, because it might save money for the authority
    D. tell the assistant to have his brother contact the project manager

2. A new custodial assistant under your supervision is waxing a floor for the first time. While the job seems to be going along well, he is not doing it quite the way you asked him to do it and so is taking longer than he should. Which of the following is the BEST action for you to take under these conditions?

    A. Leave him to finish the job and go on to the next one
    B. Interrupt him and tell him to do the job the way he was taught
    C. Tell him he is doing well but that he should do better
    D. Explain to him why your way is faster and tell him to try it

3. The easiest way for a custodian to find out how many supplies are available is to

    A. look at last year's figures
    B. keep an up-to-date inventory
    C. ask one of the men to let you know
    D. check the availability when he uses a special item

4. Of the following, the MOST likely result of a report that has been planned well is that it will

    A. explain, in detail, general procedures of supervision
    B. be read by most of the top officials of the department
    C. have some award-winning suggestions
    D. state the facts in a clear, orderly way

5. It is better to make a written report, instead of a face-to-face report, when

    A. you expect your superior to have questions about what is in the report right away
    B. your superior wants to know about your work immediately
    C. the report is very short
    D. you will have to give your report to many people in different locations

6. Of the following, the MOST important fact a custodian should include in an accident report is

   A. the name of the insurance company of the injured person
   B. cost to the city of the accident
   C. name and address of the injured person
   D. your idea for preventing such an accident in the future

7. Making an outline of the contents of a long report, before writing the report, is often a good idea. The advantage is that

   A. you can file an outline to refer to it in the future
   B. your supervisor can see it and know that you are working on the report
   C. you can make the outline a part of your report
   D. it will help you in writing the report

8. Of the following, the MOST important reason for the custodian's making detailed reports in all accidents is to

   A. have a record of who is at fault in case lawsuits should result
   B. be better able to estimate the cost of the accident
   C. reduce the number of compensation claims
   D. determine the cause of the accident and prevent future accidents

9. A custodian's written instructions to his staff on the subject of security in public buildings should include instructions to

   A. exclude the public at all times
   B. admit the public at all times
   C. admit the public only if they are neat and well-dressed
   D. admit the public during specified hours

10. The key figure in any custodial safety program is the

    A. building custodian          B. cleaner
    C. operating engineer          D. commissioner

11. A supervisor should know the equipment used in his work well enough to

    A. make any repairs which might be needed
    B. know what parts to remove in case of breakdown
    C. anticipate any reasonable possibility of a breakdown
    D. know all the lubricants specified by the manufacturer

12. The PRIMARY responsibility of a building custodian is to

    A. make friends of all subordinates
    B. search for new methods of doing the work
    C. win the respect of his superior
    D. get the work done properly within a reasonable time

13. If the directions given by your superior are not clear, the BEST thing for you to do is to

A. ask to have the directions repeated and clarified
B. proceed to do the work taking a chance on doing the right thing
C. do nothing until some later time when you can find out exactly what is wanted
D. ask one of the other men in your crew what he would do under the circumstances

14. Of the following procedures concerning grievances of subordinate personnel, the custodian-engineer should maintain an attitude on

    A. paying little attention to little grievances
    B. being very alert to grievances and make adjustments in existing conditions to appease all personnel
    C. knowing the most frequent causes of grievances and strive to prevent them from arising
    D. maintaining firm discipline of a nature that *smooths out* all grievances

15. Of the following, the BEST course of action to take to settle a dispute or conflict between two employees is to

    A. insist that the two employees settle the case between themselves
    B. call in each one separately and, after hearing their cases presented, decide the issue
    C. bring both in for a conference at the same time and make the decision in their presence
    D. have both present their points of view and arguments in written memoranda and on this basis make your decision

16. If, as a custodian-engineer, you discover an error in your report submitted to the main office, you should

    A. do nothing, since it is possible that one error will have little effect on the total report
    B. wait until the error is discovered in the main office and then offer to work overtime to correct it
    C. go directly to the supervisor in the main office after working hours and ask him unofficially to correct the error
    D. notify the main office immediately so that the error can be corrected, if necessary

17. There are a considerable number of forms and reports to be submitted on schedule by the custodian-engineer. The ADVISABLE method of accomplishing this duty is to

    A. fill out the reports at odd times during the days when you have free time
    B. schedule a definite period of the work week for completing these forms and reports
    C. assign your foreman or cleaner to handle all these forms for you and to have them available on time
    D. classify or group the forms and reports and fill out only one of each group and refer the other forms or reports to the ones completed

18. A custodian-engineer can BEST evaluate the quality of work performed by custodial personnel by

    A. periodic inspection of the building's cleanliness
    B. studying the time records of personnel
    C. reviewing the building cleaning expenditures
    D. analyzing complaints of building occupants

19. Assume that you are the custodian-engineer and one of your employees wants to talk with you about a grievance. Of the following actions, the LEAST desirable action for you to take is to

    A. listen sympathetically
    B. conduct the discussion openly in the presence of the workforce
    C. try to get his point of view
    D. endeavor to obtain all the facts

20. Of the following factors, the one which is LEAST important in evaluating an employee and his work is his

    A. dependability              B. quantity of work
    C. quality of work            D. education and training

21. Supervision of a group of people engaged in building cleaning operations should NOT include supervision of

    A. time spent in cleaning operations
    B. utilization of official rest and lunch periods
    C. cleaning methods
    D. materials used for various cleaning jobs

22. Of the following methods, the BEST one to utilize in assigning custodial personnel to clean a multi-floor school building is to

    A. allow the cleaners to pick their rooms or area assignments out of a hat
    B. have the supervisor make specific room or area assignments to each cleaner separately
    C. rotate room and area assignments daily according to a chart posted on the bulletin board
    D. let a different member of the group make the room or area assignments each week

23. Assume that you are the custodian-engineer and that you have discovered a bottle of liquor in one of your employees' locker. The BEST course of action to take is to

    A. fire him immediately
    B. explain to him that liquor should not be brought into a school building and that a repetition may result in disciplinary action
    C. suspend him until the end of the week and take him back only on a probational basis
    D. assemble the staff and tell them they are all equally guilty for not having reported the matter to you

24. Of the following items, the one which is the LEAST important in the preparation of a report is that the report

    A. is brief, but to the point
    B. uses the prescribed form if there is one
    C. contains extra copies
    D. is accurate

25. In order to have building employees willing to follow standardized cleaning and maintenance procedures, the supervisor must be prepared to

    A. work alongside the employees
    B. demonstrate the reasonableness of the procedures
    C. offer incentive pay for their utilization
    D. allow the employees the free use of the time saved by their adoption

25.____

---

## KEY (CORRECT ANSWERS)

| | | | |
|---|---|---|---|
| 1. | A | 11. | C |
| 2. | D | 12. | D |
| 3. | B | 13. | A |
| 4. | B | 14. | C |
| 5. | D | 15. | C |
| 6. | C | 16. | D |
| 7. | D | 17. | B |
| 8. | D | 18. | A |
| 9. | D | 19. | B |
| 10. | A | 20. | D |

21. B
22. B
23. B
24. C
25. B

---

# EXAMINATION SECTION
# TEST 1

DIRECTIONS: Each question or incomplete statement is followed by several suggested answers or completions. Select the one that BEST answers the question or completes the statement. *PRINT THE LETTER OF THE CORRECT ANSWER IN THE SPACE AT THE RIGHT.*

1. Of the following, the BEST way for you to make sure that a cleaner understands a spoken order which you have given to him is for you to

    A. ask him to repeat the order in his own words
    B. ask him whether he has understood the order
    C. watch how he begins to follow the order
    D. ask him whether he has any questions about the order

    1.____

2. You have called a meeting with your cleaners to get their suggestions on ways to keep up cleaning standards in spite of budget cutbacks.
You are MOST likely to be successful in encouraging them to participate in the discussion if you

    A. start the meeting by giving the cleaners all your own suggestions first
    B. keep the meeting going by talking whenever the cleaners have nothing to say
    C. get the cleaners to *think out loud* by asking them for their interpretations of the problem
    D. comment on and evaluate the suggestions made by each cleaner immediately after he makes them

    2.____

3. If a custodian knows that rumors being spread by his assistants are false, he should

    A. tell the assistants that the rumors are false
    B. tell the assistants the facts which the rumors have falsified
    C. threaten to discipline any assistant who spreads the rumors
    D. find out which assistant started the rumor and have him suspended

    3.____

4. One of your best cleaners tells you in private that he wants to quit his job.
The FIRST thing you should do in handling this matter is to

    A. ask the cleaner why he wants to quit his job
    B. tell the cleaner to take a few days to think it over
    C. refer the cleaner to the personnel office
    D. try to convince the cleaner not to quit his job

    4.____

5. The MOST important reason why a custodian should seek the suggestions of his cleaners on job-related matters is that the

    A. cleaners generally have greater knowledge of job-related matters than the custodian
    B. cleaners will tend to have a greater feeling of participation in their jobs by making suggestions
    C. custodian will be able to hold the cleaners responsible for any suggestions he follows
    D. custodian can win the respect of his cleaners by showing them the errors in their suggestions

    5.____

6. Your supervisor has ordered you to announce to your cleaners a new cleaning rule with which you disagree. You should

    A. admit honestly to your cleaners that you disagree with the rule
    B. announce the rule to your cleaners without expressing your disagreement
    C. encourage your cleaners by telling them you agree with the rule
    D. tell your supervisor that you refuse to announce any rule with which you disagree

7. Of the following, the BEST practice to follow in criticizing the work performance of a cleaner is to

    A. save up several criticisms and make them all at one time
    B. soften your criticisms by being humorous
    C. have another cleaner, who has more seniority, give the criticism
    D. make sure you explain to the cleaner the reasons for your criticism

8. The work goals which you set for your cleaners should be

    A. slightly less than their capabilities, so that they have some slack time
    B. approximately equal to their capabilities, so that they work at normal capacity
    C. slightly above their capabilities, so that they must extend themselves a little
    D. considerably above their capabilities, so that they must always be trying to catch up

9. Of the following, the BEST way to reduce unnecessary absences among your cleaners is to

    A. ask your cleaners the reason for their absence every time they are absent
    B. rely entirely on written warnings once every month to cleaners who have been absent too often during the month
    C. have your cleaners make a formal written report to you every time they are absent explaining the reason for their absence
    D. post publicly every month a list of those cleaners who you feel have been absent unnecessarily during the month

10. Of the following methods that might be used to deal with a cleaner who is habitually late for work without good reason, the BEST one for you to apply is to

    A. give the cleaner an assignment where his lateness will not inconvenience any other cleaner
    B. assign the cleaner to the most disagreeable jobs until he stops being late for work
    C. call the cleaner aside in private to give him a stern lecture on his habitual lateness
    D. appeal to the cleaner's better nature to urge him to correct his habitual lateness

11. To improve efficiency, you have instituted a new system of assigning work to your cleaners.
    Your cleaners are MOST likely to be cooperative in accepting this new system if you

    A. remind them how inefficient the former system was
    B. tell them of the advantages of the new system but not the disadvantages
    C. refuse to make any changes in the new system once you have instituted it
    D. follow-up on any problems the cleaners may have because of the new system

12. You are most likely to gain the wholehearted cooperation of your cleaners if you appeal MAINLY to their

    A. natural dislike for work
    B. fear of punishment
    C. satisfaction in a job well done
    D. desire to avoid responsibility

13. When combined with good leadership, regular inspections by a custodian of the work done by his cleaners can help create good morale MAINLY because the cleaners know that the custodian

    A. is interested in how they do their work
    B. will leave them alone between inspections
    C. may catch them if they do poor work
    D. does not rely on them to do their work unwatched

14. While you are making an inspection, you find two of your cleaners arguing angrily about the best procedure to follow in completing their assignment.
    Of the following, the FIRST thing you should do is to

    A. tell them that they will both be disciplined
    B. ignore the argument, since it is probably none of your business
    C. ask each one for his side of the argument
    D. order them to follow the procedure favored by the more experienced of the two

15. A one-person cleaning assignment which all of your cleaners find disagreeable comes up one day every month. It is BEST supervisory practice to assign

    A. each one in turn, by rotation
    B. anyone who happens to be available, by chance
    C. anyone you wish to punish for his poor work performance
    D. the one who is least likely to complain about the assignment

16. Despite your repeated warnings, one of your cleaners, through carelessness, has seriously damaged an expensive waxing machine.
    You are MOST likely to be effective in disciplining him if you

    A. reprimand him in the presence of the other cleaners
    B. consider his work record when deciding how to discipline him
    C. tell him that you will decide on a punishment for him during the following week
    D. make a point of reminding him frequently how he carelessly damaged an expensive waxing machine

17. A custodian is approached by a newspaper reporter and is asked questions about a certain member of the office staff. Of the following, the BEST course of action for the custodian to take is to

    A. ignore the newspaper reporter
    B. refer the newspaper reporter to the personnel office for information
    C. tell the newspaper reporter anything he wishes to know, but warn him that the information is not official
    D. give the newspaper reporter false information to discourage further questioning

18. While a custodian is making a note of the fluorescent lamps that need to be replaced in a waiting room, one of the waiting clients starts to complain angrily about the high cost of custodial services in the city.
    Of the following, the BEST course of action for the custodian to take is to

    A. tell the individual to be quiet and show more respect for city representatives
    B. try to persuade the person to take a more reasonable point of view
    C. listen courteously until the client has finished and then complain about the high cost of welfare
    D. ignore the comments and continue with his work

19. A group of workers complain to you about the lack of cleanliness in your building. You realize that budget cutbacks have unavoidably led to shortages in manpower and equipment for the cleaning staff.
    Of the following, the BEST way for you to answer these workers is to

    A. tell them frankly that the cleanliness of the building is none of their business
    B. apologize for the condition of the building and promise that your men will work harder
    C. tell them to take their complaints to the administration and not to you
    D. explain the reasons for the building's condition and what you are doing to improve it

20. The MOST important role of the custodian in promoting good public relations should be to help

    A. increase understanding between the custodial staff and the public which it serves
    B. keep from public attention any failings on the part of the custodial staff
    C. increase the authority of the custodial staff over the public with which it deals
    D. keep the public from interfering in the operations of the custodial staff

21. A supervisor conducting a staff meeting calls you to complain that the cleaners working in the empty office next to his are being unnecessarily noisy.
    Of the following, the BEST response to the supervisor is to tell him that

    A. he should go next door to tell the cleaners to stop the unnecessary noise
    B. you will tell the cleaners about his complaint and instruct them not to make unnecessary noise
    C. he should file a formal complaint against the cleaners with your superior
    D. you will come to his office to judge for yourself whether the cleaners are being unnecessarily noisy

22. The attitude a custodian should *generally* maintain toward the workers and office staff is one of

    A. avoidance        B. superiority
    C. courtesy         D. servility

23. A custodian notices that one of the clerks in using an unsafe electrical appliance which may cause a fire at any time.
Of the following, the BEST course of action for the custodian to take is to

    A. go into the clerk's office after hours and remove the appliance
    B. notify the fire department so that a summons will be served on the clerk
    C. go into the clerk's office after hours and damage the appliance in such a way as to eliminate the hazard
    D. speak to the clerk's supervisor privately and explain the danger and request that the supervisor ask the clerk to disconnect the appliance

23.____

24. An emergency has developed in which a custodian must enter a locked office to close some shut-off valves. The occupant of the office is a new employee who is alone and refuses to let the custodian in because she does not recognize him.
Of the following, the BEST course of action for the custodian to take is to

    A. force his way in and then apologize
    B. summon the police and explain that she is obstructing official city business
    C. show his credentials or seek out other individuals that the employee knows
    D. tell the employee that there is a fire in the building and her life is in danger

24.____

25. A telephone caller tells a building custodian that a bomb has been placed in the building and immediately hangs up the phone.
The FIRST thing the building custodian should do is to

    A. call the fire department
    B. call the police department
    C. let his subordinate handle it
    D. ignore the call, since most threats are hoaxes

25.____

## KEY (CORRECT ANSWERS)

1. A
2. C
3. B
4. A
5. B

6. B
7. D
8. C
9. A
10. C

11. D
12. C
13. A
14. C
15. A

16. B
17. B
18. D
19. D
20. A

21. B
22. C
23. D
24. C
25. B

# TEST 2

DIRECTIONS: Each question or incomplete statement is followed by several suggested answers or completions. Select the one that BEST answers the question or completes the statement. *PRINT THE LETTER OF THE CORRECT ANSWER IN THE SPACE AT THE RIGHT.*

1. Despite your repeated warnings, one of your custodial assistants, through carelessness, has seriously damaged an expensive paper shredder.
   You are MOST likely to be LEAST effective in disciplining him if you

   A. reprimand him in the presence of other custodial assistants
   B. consider his work record when deciding how to discipline him
   C. tell him that you will decide on a punishment for him during the following week
   D. make a point of reminding him now and then how he carelessly damaged an expensive paper shredder

   1.____

2. Assume that one of your custodial assistants, although he does not drink on the job, is an alcoholic whose work performance has become inadequate because of his drinking problem.
   Of the following, the BEST approach to take in dealing with this custodial assistant is to

   A. do nothing, since he does not drink on the job
   B. recommend to your supervisor that the custodial assistant be fired because he is an alcoholic
   C. counsel him on the personal and emotional problems which cause his drinking problem
   D. advise him to seek professional help for his drinking problem

   2.____

3. Of the following, you are MOST likely to be effective in training an inexperienced custodial assistant to do a complicated cleaning job if you

   A. train him in all parts of the job at the same time
   B. first demonstrate to him the most common errors in doing the job
   C. let him know from time to time how he is doing in learning the job
   D. encourage him in the beginning by overlooking any mistakes he may make

   3.____

4. Praising a trainee who is making unusually good progress in learning from your training is *generally* considered to be

   A. *desirable,* because he is likely to be encouraged to continue making good progress
   B. *undesirable,* because he is likely to become overconfident and begin to do poorly
   C. *desirable,* because the other trainees are likely to become envious and try to compete with him
   D. *undesirable,* because he should not be praised for doing his job

   4.____

5. Of the following, the MOST effective way for you to train a custodial assistant to perform a complicated cleaning job about which he has some knowledge is to

   A. let him do the entire job, then have him question you as to his problems
   B. repeat in your training what he already knows about the cleaning job
   C. teach him those parts of the job with which he is unfamiliar
   D. keep him slightly ill at ease during training

   5.____

105

6. A custodial foreman in a large building should *normally* spend the GREATEST part of his working time on

   A. work planning
   B. records and reports
   C. personnel problems
   D. supervision and inspection

7. In general, the MOST efficient method for doing a cleaning job is the method which

   A. must be repeated most frequently
   B. has the most different steps and operations
   C. gives the best results for the least amount of effort
   D. requires the efforts of the greatest number of custodial assistants

8. If the directions given by your superior are not clear, the BEST thing for you to do is to

   A. ask to have the directions repeated and clarified
   B. proceed to do the work taking a chance on doing the right thing
   C. do nothing until some later time when you can find out exactly what is wanted
   D. ask one of the other men in your crew what he would do under the circumstances

9. Of the following procedures concerning grievances of subordinate personnel, the custodian-engineer should maintain an attitude of

   A. paying little attention to little grievances
   B. being very alert to grievances and make adjustments in existing conditions to appease all personnel
   C. knowing the most frequent causes of grievances and strive to prevent them from arising
   D. maintain rigid discipline of a nature that *smooths out* all grievances

10. Of the following, the BEST course of action to take to settle a dispute or conflict between two employees is to

    A. insist that the two employees settle the case between themselves
    B. call in each one separately and, after hearing their cases presented, decide the issue
    C. bring both in for a conference at the same time and make the decision in their presence
    D. have both present their points of view and arguments in written memoranda and on this basis make your decision

11. If, as a custodian-engineer, you discover an error in your report submitted to the main office, you should

    A. do nothing, since it is possible that one error will have little effect on the total report
    B. wait until the error is discovered in the main office and then offer to work overtime to correct it
    C. go directly to the supervisor in the main office after working hours and ask him unofficially to correct the error
    D. notify the main office immediately so that the error can be corrected, if necessary

12. There are a considerable number of forms and reports to be submitted on schedule by the custodian-engineer. The ADVISABLE method of accomplishing this duty is to

    A. fill out the reports at odd times during the days when you have free time
    B. schedule a definite period of the work-week for completing these forms and reports
    C. assign your foreman or cleaner to handle all these forms for you and to have them available on time
    D. classify or group the forms and reports and fill out only one of each group and refer the other forms or reports to the ones completed

13. A custodian-engineer can BEST evaluate the quality of work performed by custodial personnel by

    A. periodic inspection of the building's cleanliness
    B. studying the time records of personnel
    C. reviewing the building cleaning expenditures
    D. analyzing complaints of building occupants

14. Assume that you are the custodian-engineer and one of your employees wants to talk with you about a grievance. Of the following actions, the LEAST desirable action for you to take is to

    A. listen sympathetically
    B. conduct the discussion openly in the presence of the work-force
    C. try to get his point of view
    D. endeavor to obtain all the facts

15. Of the following factors, the one which is LEAST important in evaluating an employee and his work is his

    A. dependability        B. quantity of work
    C. quality of work      D. education and training

16. Supervision of a group of people engaged in building cleaning operations should NOT include supervision of

    A. time spent in cleaning operations
    B. utilization of official rest and lunch periods
    C. cleaning methods
    D. materials used for various cleaning jobs

17. Of the following methods, the BEST one to utilize in assigning custodial personnel to clean a multi-floor school building is to

    A. allow the cleaners to pick their rooms or area assignments out of a hat
    B. have the supervisor make specific room or area assignments to each cleaner separately
    C. rotate room and area assignments daily according to a chart posted on the bulletin board
    D. let a different member of the group make the room or area assignments each week

18. Assume that you are the custodian-engineer and that you have discovered a bottle of liquor in one of your employees' locker.
    The BEST course of action to take is to

A. fire him immediately
B. explain to him that liquor should not be brought into a school building and that a repetition may result in disciplinary action
C. suspend him until the end of the week and take him back only on a probational basis
D. assemble the staff and tell them they are all equally guilty for not having reported the matter to you

19. Of the following items, the one which is the LEAST important in the preparation of a report is that the report

    A. is brief, but to the point
    B. uses the prescribed form if there is one
    C. contains extra copies
    D. is accurate

20. In order to have building employees willing to follow standardized cleaning and maintenance procedures, the supervisor must be prepared to

    A. work alongside the employees
    B. demonstrate the reasonableness of the procedures
    C. offer incentive pay for their utilization
    D. allow the employees the free use of the time saved by their adoption

21. A fireman is frequently late in taking over his shift. In considering this situation, the factor which is of LEAST importance is

    A. the reason for his lateness
    B. how his lateness affects the work of other firemen
    C. how often he is late
    D. how willing he is to do emergency work

22. Suppose that you are preparing a requisition for cleaning supplies for the school year. The BEST single method of estimating the amount to be ordered is to

    A. ask each cleaner to submit an estimate of his needs for the coming year
    B. call other custodian-engineers to obtain from them an estimate of supply requirements
    C. confer with the school principal to obtain his estimate of school cleaning supply needs
    D. review the records of supplies used during the last few years

23. A number of injuries to pupils have occurred while they were traveling on the stairs of the school. Your inspection shows no defects or inadequacy of lighting.
    The MOST desirable step to take to reduce the frequency of these accidents is to

    A. assign a cleaner to each stairway during the time the children use them
    B. put up signs warning the children to be careful
    C. suggest to the school principal that his teaching staff discuss the matter with the children
    D. install better lighting on the stairs and make certain that handrails are in perfect condition

24. The custodian-engineer, to be effective and efficient, must budget his time. This means MOST NEARLY that

    A. a value in dollars and costs should be placed on each hour's work of a custodian-engineer
    B. the custodian-engineer should make certain that all of his time, as well as that of his employees, is accounted for
    C. a time schedule for each employee must be prepared so that the yearly allowance for the school is not exceeded
    D. the custodian-engineer should plan his jobs and duties so that all can be covered as required

25. Suppose that a cleaner has been found to be quite negligent in his work and has been warned repeatedly by you.
    If you find that your warnings have not changed the man's attitude or work habits, the PROPER thing to do is to

    A. have the employee discharged
    B. change his assignment in the school to a less desirable job
    C. have a serious talk with the cleaner to find out why he does not do satisfactory work
    D. give the cleaner a final warning

## KEY (CORRECT ANSWERS)

| | | | |
|---|---|---|---|
| 1. | A | 11. | D |
| 2. | D | 12. | B |
| 3. | C | 13. | A |
| 4. | A | 14. | B |
| 5. | C | 15. | D |
| 6. | D | 16. | B |
| 7. | C | 17. | B |
| 8. | A | 18. | B |
| 9. | C | 19. | C |
| 10. | C | 20. | B |

21. D
22. D
23. C
24. D
25. A

# PHILOSOPHY, PRINCIPLES, PRACTICES, AND TECHNICS
# OF
# SUPERVISION, ADMINISTRATION, MANAGEMENT, AND ORGANIZATION

## TABLE OF CONTENTS

| | Page |
|---|---|
| MEANING OF SUPERVISION | 1 |
| THE OLD AND THE NEW SUPERVISION | 1 |
| THE EIGHT (8) BASIC PRINCIPLES OF THE NEW SUPERVISION | 1 |
|     I. Principle of Responsibility | 1 |
|     II. Principle of Authority | 2 |
|     III. Principle of Self-Growth | 2 |
|     IV. Principle of Individual Worth | 2 |
|     V. Principle of Creative Leadership | 2 |
|     VI. Principle of Success and Failure | 2 |
|     VII. Principle of Science | 3 |
|     VIII. Principle of Cooperation | 3 |
| WHAT IS ADMINISTRATION? | 3 |
|     I. Practices Commonly Classed as "Supervisory" | 3 |
|     II. Practices Commonly Classed as "Administrative" | 3 |
|     III. Practices Commonly Classed as Both "Supervisory" and "Administrative" | 4 |
| RESPONSIBILITIES OF THE SUPERVISOR | 4 |
| COMPETENCIES OF THE SUPERVISOR | 4 |
| THE PROFESSIONAL SUPERVISOR-EMPLOYEE RELATIONSHIP | 4 |
| MINI-TEXT IN SUPERVISION, ADMINISTRATION, MANAGEMENT, AND ORGANIZATION | 5 |
|     I. Brief Highlights | 5 |
|         A. Levels of Management | 6 |
|         B. What the Supervisor Must Learn | 6 |
|         C. A Definition of Supervision | 6 |
|         D. Elements of the Team Concept | 6 |
|         E. Principles of Organization | 6 |
|         F. The Four Important Parts of Every Job | 7 |
|         G. Principles of Delegation | 7 |
|         H. Principles of Effective Communications | 7 |
|         I. Principles of Work Improvement | 7 |
|         J. Areas of Job Improvement | 7 |
|         K. Seven Key Points in Making Improvements | 8 |

|     |     |                                              |     |
| --- | --- | -------------------------------------------- | --- |
|     | L.  | Corrective Techniques for Job Improvement    | 8   |
|     | M.  | A Planning Checklist                         | 8   |
|     | N.  | Five Characteristics of Good Directions      | 9   |
|     | O.  | Types of Directions                          | 9   |
|     | P.  | Controls                                     | 9   |
|     | Q.  | Orienting the New Employee                   | 9   |
|     | R.  | Checklist for Orienting New Employees        | 9   |
|     | S.  | Principles of Learning                       | 10  |
|     | T.  | Causes of Poor Performance                   | 10  |
|     | U.  | Four Major Steps in On-the-Job Instructions  | 10  |
|     | V.  | Employees Want Five Things                   | 10  |
|     | W.  | Some Don'ts in Regard to Praise              | 11  |
|     | X.  | How to Gain Your Workers' Confidence         | 11  |
|     | Y.  | Sources of Employee Problems                 | 11  |
|     | Z.  | The Supervisor's Key to Discipline           | 11  |
|     | AA. | Five Important Processes of Management       | 12  |
|     | BB. | When the Supervisor Fails to Plan            | 12  |
|     | CC. | Fourteen General Principles of Management    | 12  |
|     | DD. | Change                                       | 12  |

II. Brief Topical Summaries 13
    A. Who/What is the Supervisor? 13
    B. The Sociology of Work 13
    C. Principles and Practices of Supervision 14
    D. Dynamic Leadership 14
    E. Processes for Solving Problems 15
    F. Training for Results 15
    G. Health, Safety, and Accident Prevention 16
    H. Equal Employment Opportunity 16
    I. Improving Communications 16
    J. Self-Development 17
    K. Teaching and Training 17
        1. The Teaching Process 17
            a. Preparation 17
            b. Presentation 18
            c. Summary 18
            d. Application 18
            e. Evaluation 18
        2. Teaching Methods 18
            a. Lecture 18
            b. Discussion 18
            c. Demonstration 19
            d. Performance 19
            e. Which Method to Use 19

# PHILOSOPHY, PRINCIPLES, PRACTICES, AND TECHNICS OF SUPERVISION, ADMINISTRATION, MANAGEMENT, AND ORGANIZATION

## MEANING OF SUPERVISION

The extension of the democratic philosophy has been accompanied by an extension in the scope of supervision. Modern leaders and supervisors no longer think of supervision in the narrow sense of being confined chiefly to visiting employees, supplying materials, or rating the staff. They regard supervision as being intimately related to all the concerned agencies of society, they speak of the supervisor's function in terms of "growth," rather than the "improvement" of employees.

This modern concept of supervision may be defined as follows: Supervision is leadership and the development of leadership within groups which are cooperatively engaged in inspection, research, training, guidance, and evaluation.

## THE OLD AND THE NEW SUPERVISION

### TRADITIONAL
1. Inspection
2. Focused on the employee
3. Visitation
4. Random and haphazard
5. Imposed and authoritarian
6. One person usually

### MODERN
1. Study and analysis
2. Focused on aims, materials, methods, supervisors, employees, environment
3. Demonstrations, intervisitation, workshops, directed reading, bulletins, etc.
4. Definitely organized and planned (scientific)
5. Cooperative and democratic
6. Many persons involved (creative)

## THE EIGHT (8) BASIC PRINCIPLES OF THE NEW SUPERVISION

I. Principle of Responsibility
   Authority to act and responsibility for acting must be joined.
   A. If you give responsibility, give authority.
   B. Define employee duties clearly.
   C. Protect employees from criticism by others.
   D. Recognize the rights as well as obligations of employees.
   E. Achieve the aims of a democratic society insofar as it is possible within the area of your work.
   F. Establish a situation favorable to training and learning.
   G. Accept ultimate responsibility for everything done in your section, unit, office, division, department.
   H. Good administration and good supervision are inseparable.

II. Principle of Authority
The success of the supervisor is measured by the extent to which the power of authority is not used.
   A. Exercise simplicity and informality in supervision
   B. Use the simplest machinery of supervision
   C. If it is good for the organization as a whole, it is probably justified.
   D. Seldom be arbitrary or authoritative.
   E. Do not base your work on the power of position or of personality.
   F. Permit and encourage the free expression of opinions.

III. Principle of Self-Growth
The success of the supervisor is measured by the extent to which, and the speed with which, he is no longer needed.
   A. Base criticism on principles, not on specifics.
   B. Point out higher activities to employees.
   C. Train for self-thinking by employees to meet new situations.
   D. Stimulate initiative, self-reliance, and individual responsibility
   E. Concentrate on stimulating the growth of employees rather than on removing defects.

IV. Principle of Individual Worth
Respect for the individual is a paramount consideration in supervision.
   A. Be human and sympathetic in dealing with employees.
   B. Don't nag about things to be done.
   C. Recognize the individual differences among employees and seek opportunities to permit best expression of each personality.

V. Principle of Creative Leadership
The best supervision is that which is not apparent to the employee.
   A. Stimulate, don't drive employees to creative action.
   B. Emphasize doing good things.
   C. Encourage employees to do what they do best.
   D. Do not be too greatly concerned with details of subject or method.
   E. Do not be concerned exclusively with immediate problems and activities.
   F. Reveal higher activities and make them both desired and maximally possible.
   G. Determine procedures in the light of each situation but see that these are derived from a sound basic philosophy.
   H. Aid, inspire, and lead so as to liberate the creative spirit latent in all good employees.

VI. Principle of Success and Failure
There are no unsuccessful employees, only unsuccessful supervisors who have failed to give proper leadership.
   A. Adapt suggestions to the capacities, attitudes, and prejudices of employees.
   B. Be gradual, be progressive, be persistent.
   C. Help the employee find the general principle; have the employee apply his own problem to the general principle.
   D. Give adequate appreciation for good work and honest effort.
   E. Anticipate employee difficulties and help to prevent them.
   F. Encourage employees to do the desirable things they will do anyway.
   G. Judge your supervision by the results it secures.

VII. Principle of Science
Successful supervision is scientific, objective, and experimental. It is based on facts, not on prejudices.
   A. Be cumulative in results.
   B. Never divorce your suggestions from the goals of training.
   C. Don't be impatient of results.
   D. Keep all matters on a professional, not a personal, level.
   E. Do not be concerned exclusively with immediate problems and activities.
   F. Use objective means of determining achievement and rating where possible.

VIII. Principle of Cooperation
Supervision is a cooperative enterprise between supervisor and employee.
   A. Begin with conditions as they are.
   B. Ask opinions of all involved when formulating policies.
   C. Organization is as good as its weakest link.
   D. Let employees help to determine policies and department programs.
   E. Be approachable and accessible—physically and mentally.
   F. Develop pleasant social relationships.

## WHAT IS ADMINISTRATION

Administration is concerned with providing the environment, the material facilities, and the operational procedures that will promote the maximum growth and development of supervisors and employees. (Organization is an aspect and a concomitant of administration.)

There is no sharp line of demarcation between supervision and administration; these functions are intimately interrelated and, often, overlapping. They are complementary activities.

I. Practices Commonly Classed as "Supervisory"
   A. Conducting employees' conferences
   B. Visiting sections, units, offices, divisions, departments
   C. Arranging for demonstrations
   D. Examining plans
   E. Suggesting professional reading
   F. Interpreting bulletins
   G. Recommending in-service training courses
   H. Encouraging experimentation
   I. Appraising employee morale
   J. Providing for intervisitation

II. Practices Commonly Classified as "Administrative"
   A. Management of the office
   B. Arrangement of schedules for extra duties
   C. Assignment of rooms or areas
   D. Distribution of supplies
   E. Keeping records and reports
   F. Care of audio-visual materials
   G. Keeping inventory records
   H. Checking record cards and books

      I. Programming special activities
      J. Checking on the attendance and punctuality of employees

III. Practices Commonly Classified as Both "Supervisory" and "Administrative"
    A. Program construction
    B. Testing or evaluating outcomes
    C. Personnel accounting
    D. Ordering instructional materials

## RESPONSIBILITIES OF THE SUPERVISOR

A person employed in a supervisory capacity must constantly be able to improve his own efficiency and ability. He represent the employer to the employees and only continuous self-examination can make him a capable supervisor.

Leadership and training are the supervisor's responsibility. An efficient working unit is one in which the employees work with the supervisor. It is his job to bring out the best in his employees. He must always be relaxed, courteous, and calm in his association with his employees. Their feelings are important, and a harsh attitude does not develop the most efficient employees.

## COMPETENCES OF THE SUPERVISOR

    I. Complete knowledge of the duties and responsibilities of his position.
    II. To be able to organize a job, plan ahead, and carry through.
    III. To have self-confidence and initiative.
    IV. To be able to handle the unexpected situation and make quick decisions.
    V. To be able to properly train subordinates in the positions they are best suited for.
    VI. To be able to keep good human relations among his subordinates.
    VII. To be able to keep good human relations between his subordinates and himself and to earn their respect and trust.

## THE PROFESSIONAL SUPERVISOR-EMPLOYEE RELATIONSHIP

There are two kinds of efficiency: one kind is only apparent and is produced in organizations through the exercise of mere discipline; this is but a simulation of the second, or true, efficiency which springs from spontaneous cooperation. If you are a manager, no matter how great or small your responsibility, it is your job, in the final analysis, to create and develop this involuntary cooperation among the people whom you supervise. For, no matter how powerful a combination of money, machines, and materials a company may have, this is a dead and sterile thing without a team of willing, thinking, and articulate people to guide it.

The following 21 points are presented as indicative of the exemplary basic relationship that should exist between supervisor and employee:

1. Each person wants to be liked and respected by his fellow employee and wants to be treated with consideration and respect by his superior.
2. The most competent employee will make an error. However, in a unit where good relations exist between the supervisor and his employees, tenseness and fear do not exist. Thus, errors are not hidden or covered up, and the efficiency of a unit is not impaired.

3. Subordinates resent rules, regulations, or orders that are unreasonable or unexplained.
4. Subordinates are quick to resent unfairness, harshness, injustices, and favoritism.
5. An employee will accept responsibility if he knows that he will be complimented for a job well done, and not too harshly chastised for failure; that his supervisor will check the cause of the failure, and, if it was the supervisor's fault, he will assume the blame therefore. If it was the employee's fault, his supervisor will explain the correct method or means of handling the responsibility.
6. An employee wants to receive credit for a suggestion he has made, that is used. If a suggestion cannot be used, the employee is entitled to an explanation. The supervisor should not say "no" and close the subject.
7. Fear and worry slow up a worker's ability. Poor working environment can impair his physical and mental health. A good supervisor avoids forceful methods, threats, and arguments to get a job done.
8. A forceful supervisor is able to train his employees individually and as a team, and is able to motivate them in the proper channels.
9. A mature supervisor is able to properly evaluate his subordinates and to keep them happy and satisfied.
10. A sensitive supervisor will never patronize his subordinates.
11. A worthy supervisor will respect his employees' confidences.
12. Definite and clear-cut responsibilities should be assigned to each executive.
13. Responsibility should always be coupled with corresponding authority.
14. No change should be made in the scope or responsibilities of a position without a definite understanding to that effect on the part of all persons concerned.
15. No executive or employee, occupying a single position in the organization, should be subject to definite orders from more than one source.
16. Orders should never be given to subordinates over the head of a responsible executive. Rather than do this, the officer in question should be supplanted.
17. Criticisms of subordinates should, whoever possible, be made privately, and in no case should a subordinate be criticized in the presence of executives or employees of equal or lower rank.
18. No dispute or difference between executives or employees as to authority or responsibilities should be considered too trivial for prompt and careful adjudication.
19. Promotions, wage changes, and disciplinary action should always be approved by the executive immediately superior to the one directly responsible.
20. No executive or employee should ever be required, or expected, to be at the same time an assistant to, and critic of, another.
21. Any executive whose work is subject to regular inspection should, wherever practicable, be given the assistance and facilities necessary to enable him to maintain an independent check of the quality of his work.

**MINI-TEXT IN SUPERVISION, ADMINISTRATION, MANAGEMENT, AND ORGANIZATION**

I. Brief Highlights

Listed concisely and sequentially are major headings and important data in the field for quick recall and review.

A. Levels of Management
Any organization of some size has several levels of management. In terms of a ladder, the levels are:

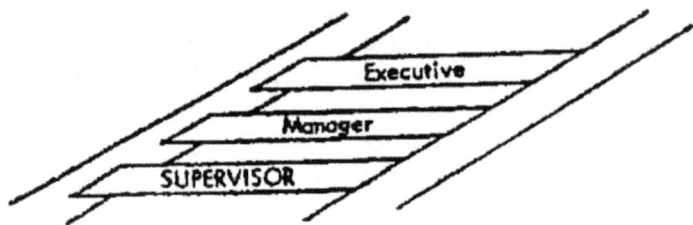

The first level is very important because it is the beginning point of management leadership.

B. What the Supervisor Must Learn
A supervisor must learn to:
1. Deal with people and their differences
2. Get the job done through people
3. Recognize the problems when they exist
4. Overcome obstacles to good performance
5. Evaluate the performance of people
6. Check his own performance in terms of accomplishment

C. A Definition of Supervisor
The term supervisor means any individual having authority, in the interests of the employer, to hire, transfer, suspend, lay-off, recall, promote, discharge, assign, reward, or discipline other employees or responsibility to direct them, or to adjust their grievances, or effectively to recommend such action, if, in connection with the foregoing, exercise of such authority is not of a merely routine or clerical nature but requires the use of independent judgment.

D. Elements of the Team Concept
What is involved in teamwork? The component parts are:
1. Members
2. A leader
3. Goals
4. Plans
5. Cooperation
6. Spirit

E. Principles of Organization
1. A team member must know what his job is.
2. Be sure that the nature and scope of a job are understood.
3. Authority and responsibility should be carefully spelled out.
4. A supervisor should be permitted to make the maximum number of decisions affecting his employees.
5. Employees should report to only one supervisor.
6. A supervisor should direct only as many employees as he can handle effectively.
7. An organization plan should be flexible.

8. Inspection and performance of work should be separate.
9. Organizational problems should receive immediate attention.
10. Assign work in line with ability and experience.

F. The Four Important Parts of Every Job
1. Inherent in every job is the *accountability* for results.
2. A second set of factors in every job is *responsibilities*.
3. Along with duties and responsibilities one must have the *authority* to act within certain limits without obtaining permission to proceed.
4. No job exists in a vacuum. The supervisor is surrounded by key *relationships*.

G. Principles of Delegation
Where work is delegated for the first time, the supervisor should think in terms of these questions:
1. Who is best qualified to do this?
2. Can an employee improve his abilities by doing this?
3. How long should an employee spend on this?
4. Are there any special problems for which he will need guidance?
5. How broad a delegation can I make?

H. Principles of Effective Communications
1. Determine the media.
2. To whom directed?
3. Identification and source authority.
4. Is communication understood?

I. Principles of Work Improvement
1. Most people usually do only the work which is assigned to them.
2. Workers are likely to fit assigned work into the time available to perform it.
3. A good workload usually stimulates output.
4. People usually do their best work when they know that results will be reviewed or inspected.
5. Employees usually feel that someone else is responsible for conditions of work, workplace layout, job methods, type of tools/equipment, and other such factors.
6. Employees are usually defensive about their job security.
7. Employees have natural resistance to change.
8. Employees can support or destroy a supervisor.
9. A supervisor usually earns the respect of his people through his personal example of diligence and efficiency.

J. Areas of Job Improvement
The areas of job improvement are quite numerous, but the most common ones which a supervisor can identify and utilize are:
1. Departmental layout
2. Flow of work
3. Workplace layout
4. Utilization of manpower
5. Work methods
6. Materials handling

7. Utilization
8. Motion economy

K. Seven Key Points in Making Improvements
1. Select the job to be improved
2. Study how it is being done now
3. Question the present method
4. Determine actions to be taken
5. Chart proposed method
6. Get approval and apply
7. Solicit worker participation

l. Corrective Techniques of Job Improvement
Specific Problems
1. Size of workload
2. Inability to meet schedules
3. Strain and fatigue
4. Improper use of men and skills
5. Waste, poor quality, unsafe conditions
6. Bottleneck conditions that hinder output
7. Poor utilization of equipment and machine
8. Efficiency and productivity of labor

General Improvement
1. Departmental layout
2. Flow of work
3. Work plan layout
4. Utilization of manpower
5. Work methods
6. Materials handling
7. Utilization of equipment
8. Motion economy

Corrective Techniques
1. Study with scale model
2. Flow chart study
3. Motion analysis
4. Comparison of units produced to standard allowance
5. Methods analysis
6. Flow chart and equipment study
7. Down time vs. running time
8. Motion analysis

M. A Planning Checklist
1. Objectives
2. Controls
3. Delegations
4. Communications
5. Resources
6. Manpower

7. Equipment
8. Supplies and materials
9. Utilization of time
10. Safety
11. Money
12. Work
13. Timing of improvements

N. Five Characteristics of Good Directions
In order to get results, directions must be:
1. Possible of accomplishment
2. Agreeable with worker interests
3. Related to mission
4. Planned and complete
5. Unmistakably clear

O. Types of Directions
1. Demands or direct orders
2. Requests
3. Suggestion or implication
4. volunteering

P. Controls
A typical listing of the overall areas in which the supervisor should establish controls might be:
1. Manpower
2. Materials
3. Quality of work
4. Quantity of work
5. Time
6. Space
7. Money
8. Methods

Q. Orienting the New Employee
1. Prepare for him
2. Welcome the new employee
3. Orientation for the job
4. Follow-up

R. Checklist for Orienting New Employees                                Yes    No
1. Do you appreciate the feelings of new employees
   when they first report for work?                                      ___    ___
2. Are you aware of the fact that the new employee must
   make a big adjustment to his job?                                     ___    ___
3. Have you given him good reasons for liking the job and
   the organization?                                                     ___    ___
4. Have you prepared for his first day on the job?                       ___    ___
5. Did you welcome him cordially and make him feel needed?               ___    ___

|   |   | Yes | No |
|---|---|---|---|

6. Did you establish rapport with him so that he feels free to talk and discuss matters with you? ___ ___
7. Did you explain his job to him and his relationship to you? ___ ___
8. Does he know that his work will be evaluated periodically on a basis that is fair and objective? ___ ___
9. Did you introduce him to his fellow workers in such a way that they are likely to accept him? ___ ___
10. Does he know what employee benefits he will receive? ___ ___
11. Does he understand the importance of being on the job and what to do if he must leave his duty station? ___ ___
12. Has he been impressed with the importance of accident prevention and safe practice? ___ ___
13. Does he generally know his way around the department? ___ ___
14. Is he under the guidance of a sponsor who will teach the right way of doing things? ___ ___
15. Do you plan to follow-up so that he will continue to adjust successfully to his job? ___ ___

S. Principles of Learning
  1. Motivation
  2. Demonstration or explanation
  3. Practice

T. Causes of Poor Performance
  1. Improper training for job
  2. Wrong tools
  3. Inadequate directions
  4. Lack of supervisory follow-up
  5. Poor communications
  6. Lack of standards of performance
  7. Wrong work habits
  8. Low morale
  9. Other

U. Four Major Steps in On-The-Job Instruction
  1. Prepare the worker
  2. Present the operation
  3. Tryout performance
  4. Follow-up

V. Employees Want Five Things
  1. Security
  2. Opportunity
  3. Recognition
  4. Inclusion
  5. Expression

W. Some Don'ts in Regard to Praise
1. Don't praise a person for something he hasn't done.
2. Don't praise a person unless you can be sincere.
3. Don't be sparing in praise just because your superior withholds it from you.
4. Don't let too much time elapse between good performance and recognition of it

X. How to Gain Your Workers' Confidence
Methods of developing confidence include such things as:
1. Knowing the interests, habits, hobbies of employees
2. Admitting your own inadequacies
3. Sharing and telling of confidence in others
4. Supporting people when they are in trouble
5. Delegating matters that can be well handled
6. Being frank and straightforward about problems and working conditions
7. Encouraging others to bring their problems to you
8. Taking action on problems which impede worker progress

Y. Sources of Employee Problems
On-the-job causes might be such things as:
1. A feeling that favoritism is exercised in assignments
2. Assignment of overtime
3. An undue amount of supervision
4. Changing methods or systems
5. Stealing of ideas or trade secrets
6. Lack of interest in job
7. Threat of reduction in force
8. Ignorance or lack of communications
9. Poor equipment
10. Lack of knowing how supervisor feels toward employee
11. Shift assignments

Off-the-job problems might have to do with:
1. Health
2. Finances
3. Housing
4. Family

Z. The Supervisor's Key to Discipline
There are several key points about discipline which the supervisor should keep in mind:
1. Job discipline is one of the disciplines of life and is directed by the supervisor.
2. It is more important to correct an employee fault than to fix blame for it.
3. Employee performance is affected by problems both on the job and off.
4. Sudden or abrupt changes in behavior can be indications of important employee problems.
5. Problems should be dealt with as soon as possible after they are identified.
6. The attitude of the supervisor may have more to do with solving problems than the techniques of problem solving.
7. Correction of employee behavior should be resorted to only after the supervisor is sure that training or counseling will not be helpful.

8. Be sure to document your disciplinary actions.
9. Make sure that you are disciplining on the basis of facts rather than personal feelings.
10. Take each disciplinary step in order, being careful not to make snap judgments, or decisions based on impatience.

AA. Five Important Processes of Management
1. Planning
2. Organizing
3. Scheduling
4. Controlling
5. Motivating

BB. When the Supervisor Fails to Plan
1. Supervisor creates impression of not knowing his job
2. May lead to excessive overtime
3. Job runs itself—supervisor lacks control
4. Deadlines and appointments missed
5. Parts of the work go undone
6. Work interrupted by emergencies
7. Sets a bad example
8. Uneven workload creates peaks and valleys
9. Too much time on minor details at expense of more important tasks

CC. Fourteen General Principles of Management
1. Division of work
2. Authority and responsibility
3. Discipline
4. Unity of command
5. Unity of direction
6. Subordination of individual interest to general interest
7. Remuneration of personnel
8. Centralization
9. Scalar chain
10. Order
11. Equity
12. Stability of tenure of personnel
13. Initiative
14. Esprit de corps

DD. Change

Bringing about change is perhaps attempted more often, and yet less well understood, than anything else the supervisor does. How do people generally react to change? (People tend to resist change that is imposed upon them by other individuals or circumstances.

Change is characteristic of every situation. It is a part of every real endeavor where the efforts of people are concerned.

1. Why do people resist change?
   People may resist change because of:
   a. Fear of the unknown
   b. Implied criticism
   c. Unpleasant experiences in the past
   d. Fear of loss of status
   e. Threat to the ego
   f. Fear of loss of economic stability

2. How can we best overcome the resistance to change?
   In initiating change, take these steps:
   a. Get ready to sell
   b. Identify sources of help
   c. Anticipate objections
   d. Sell benefits
   e. Listen in depth
   f. Follow up

II. Brief Topical Summaries

   A. Who/What is the Supervisor?
      1. The supervisor is often called the "highest level employee and the lowest level manager."
      2. A supervisor is a member of both management and the work group. He acts as a bridge between the two.
      3. Most problems in supervision are in the area of human relations, or people problems.
      4. Employees expect: Respect, opportunity to learn and to advance, and a sense of belonging, and so forth.
      5. Supervisors are responsible for directing people and organizing work. Planning is of paramount importance.
      6. A position description is a set of duties and responsibilities inherent to a given position.
      7. It is important to keep the position description up-to-date and to provide each employee with his own copy.

   B. The Sociology of Work
      1. People are alike in many ways; however, each individual is unique.
      2. The supervisor is challenged in getting to know employee differences. Acquiring skills in evaluating individuals is an asset.
      3. Maintaining meaningful working relationships in the organization is of great importance.
      4. The supervisor has an obligation to help individuals to develop to their fullest potential.
      5. Job rotation on a planned basis helps to build versatility and to maintain interest and enthusiasm in work groups.
      6. Cross training (job rotation) provides backup skills.

7. The supervisor can help reduce tension by maintaining a sense of humor, providing guidance to employees, and by making reasonable and timely decisions. Employees respond favorably to working under reasonably predictable circumstances.
8. Change is characteristic of all managerial behavior. The supervisor must adjust to changes in procedures, new methods, technological changes, and to a number of new and sometimes challenging situations.
9. To overcome the natural tendency for people to resist change, the supervisor should become more skillful in initiating change.

C. Principles and Practices of Supervision
1. Employees should be required to answer to only one superior.
2. A supervisor can effectively direct only a limited number of employees, depending upon the complexity, variety, and proximity of the jobs involved.
3. The organizational chart presents the organization in graphic form. It reflects lines of authority and responsibility as well as interrelationships of units within the organization.
4. Distribution of work can be improved through an analysis using the "Work Distribution Chart."
5. The "Work Distribution Chart" reflects the division of work within a unit in understandable form.
6. When related tasks are given to an employee, he has a better chance of increasing his skills through training.
7. The individual who is given the responsibility for tasks must also be given the appropriate authority to insure adequate results.
8. The supervisor should delegate repetitive, routine work. Preparation of recurring reports, maintaining leave and attendance records are some examples.
9. Good discipline is essential to good task performance. Discipline is reflected in the actions of employees on the job in the absence of supervision.
10. Disciplinary action may have to be taken when the positive aspects of discipline have failed. Reprimand, warning, and suspension are examples of disciplinary action.
11. If a situation calls for a reprimand, be sure it is deserved and remember it is to be done in private.

D. Dynamic Leadership
1. A style is a personal method or manner of exerting influence.
2. Authoritarian leaders often see themselves as the source of power and authority.
3. The democratic leader often perceives the group as the source of authority and power.
4. Supervisors tend to do better when using the pattern of leadership that is most natural for them.
5. Social scientists suggest that the effective supervisor use the leadership style that best fits the problem or circumstances involved.
6. All four styles—telling, selling, consulting, joining—have their place. Using one does not preclude using the other at another time.

7. The theory X point of view assumes that the average person dislikes work, will avoid it whenever possible, and must be coerced to achieve organizational objectives.
8. The theory Y point of view assumes that the average person considers work to be a natural as play, and, when the individual is committed, he requires little supervision or direction to accomplish desired objectives.
9. The leader's basic assumptions concerning human behavior and human nature affect his actions, decisions, and other managerial practices.
10. Dissatisfaction among employees is often present, but difficult to isolate. The supervisor should seek to weaken dissatisfaction by keeping promises, being sincere and considerate, keeping employees informed, and so forth.
11. Constructive suggestions should be encouraged during the natural progress of the work.

E. Processes for Solving Problems
1. People find their daily tasks more meaningful and satisfying when they can improve them.
2. The causes of problems, or the key factors, are often hidden in the background. Ability to solve problems often involves the ability to isolate them from their backgrounds. There is some substance to the cliché that some persons "can't see the forest for the trees."
3. New procedures are often developed from old ones. Problems should be broken down into manageable parts. New ideas can be adapted from old one.
4. People think differently in problem-solving situations. Using a logical, patterned approach is often useful. One approach found to be useful includes these steps:
    a. Define the problem
    b. Establish objectives
    c. Get the facts
    d. Weigh and decide
    e. Take action
    f. Evaluate action

F. Training for Results
1. Participants respond best when they feel training is important to them.
2. The supervisor has responsibility for the training and development of those who report to him.
3. When training is delegated to others, great care must be exercised to insure the trainer has knowledge, aptitude, and interest for his work as a trainer.
4. Training (learning) of some type goes on continually. The most successful supervisor makes certain the learning contributes in a productive manner to operational goals.
5. New employees are particularly susceptible to training. Older employees facing new job situations require specific training, as well as having need for development and growth opportunities.
6. Training needs require continuous monitoring.
7. The training officer of an agency is a professional with a responsibility to assist supervisors in solving training problems.

8. Many of the self-development steps important to the supervisor's own growth are equally important to the development of peers and subordinates. Knowledge of these is important when the supervisor consults with others on development and growth opportunities.

G. Health, Safety, and Accident Prevention
1. Management-minded supervisors take appropriate measures to assist employees in maintaining health and in assuring safe practices in the work environment.
2. Effective safety training and practices help to avoid injury and accidents.
3. Safety should be a management goal. All infractions of safety which are observed should be corrected without exception.
4. Employees' safety attitude, training and instruction, provision of safe tools and equipment, supervision, and leadership are considered highly important factors which contribute to safety and which can be influenced directly by supervisors.
5. When accidents do occur, they should be investigated promptly for very important reasons, including the fact that information which is gained can be used to prevent accidents in the future.

H. Equal Employment Opportunity
1. The supervisor should endeavor to treat all employees fairly, without regard to religion, race, sex, or national origin.
2. Groups tend to reflect the attitude of the leader. Prejudice can be detected even in very subtle form. Supervisors must strive to create a feeling of mutual respect and confidence in every employee.
3. Complete utilization of all human resources is a national goal. Equitable consideration should be accorded women in the work force, minority-group members, the physically and mentally handicapped, and the older employee. The important question is: "Who can do the job?"
4. Training opportunities, recognition for performance, overtime assignments, promotional opportunities, and all other personnel actions are to be handled on an equitable basis.

I. Improving Communications
1. Communications is achieving understanding between the sender and the receiver of a message. It also means sharing information—the creation of understanding.
2. Communication is basic to all human activity. Words are means of conveying meanings; however, real meanings are in people.
3. There are very practical differences in the effectiveness of one-way, impersonal, and two-way communications. Words spoken face-to-face are better understood. Telephone conversations are effective, but lack the rapport of person-to-person exchanges. The whole person communicates.
4. Cooperation and communication in an organization go hand in hand. When there is a mutual respect between people, spelling out rules and procedures for communicating is unnecessary.
5. There are several barriers to effective communications. These include failure to listen with respect and understanding, lack of skill in feedback, and misinterpreting the meanings of words used by the speaker. It is also common

practice to listen to what we want to hear, and tune out things we do not want to hear.
6. Communication is management's chief problem. The supervisor should accept the challenge to communicate more effectively and to improve interagency and intra-agency communications.
7. The supervisor may often plan for and conduct meetings. The planning phase is critical and may determine the success or the failure of a meeting.
8. Speaking before groups usually requires extra effort. Stage fright may never disappear completely, but it can be controlled.

J. Self-Development
1. Every employee is responsible for his own self-development.
2. Toastmaster and toastmistress clubs offer opportunities to improve skills in oral communications.
3. Planning for one's own self-development is of vital importance. Supervisors know their own strengths and limitations better than anyone else.
4. Many opportunities are open to aid the supervisor in his developmental efforts, including job assignments; training opportunities, both governmental and non-governmental—to include universities and professional conferences and seminars.
5. Programmed instruction offers a means of studying at one's own rate.
6. Where difficulties may arise from a supervisor's being away from his work for training, he may participate in televised home study or correspondence courses to meet his self-development needs.

K. Teaching and Training
1. The Teaching Process
Teaching is encouraging and guiding the learning activities of students toward established goals. In most cases this process consists of five steps: preparation, presentation, summarization, evaluation, and application.

   a. Preparation
   Preparation is two-fold in nature; that of the supervisor and the employee. Preparation by the supervisor is absolutely essential to success. He must know what, when, where, how, and whom he will teach. Some of the factors that should be considered are:
   1) The objectives
   2) The materials needed
   3) The methods to be used
   4) Employee participation
   5) Employee interest
   6) Training aids
   7) Evaluation
   8) Summarization

   Employee preparation consists in preparing the employee to receive the material. Probably the most important single factor in the preparation of the employee is arousing and maintaining his interest. He must know the objectives of the training, why he is there, how the material can be used, and its importance to him.

b. Presentation
In presentation, have a carefully designed plan and follow it. The plan should be accurate and complete, yet flexible enough to meet situations as they arise. The method of presentation will be determined by the particular situation and objectives.

c. Summary
A summary should be made at the end of every training unit and program. In addition, there may be internal summaries depending on the nature of the material being taught. The important thing is that the trainee must always be able to understand how each part of the new material relates to the whole.

d. Application
The supervisor must arrange work so the employee will be given a chance to apply new knowledge or skills while the material is still clear in his mind and interest is high. The trainee does not really know whether he has learned the material until he has been given a chance to apply it. If the material is not applied, it loses most of its value.

e. Evaluation
The purpose of all training is to promote learning. To determine whether the training has been a success or failure, the supervisor must evaluate this learning.
In the broadest sense, evaluation includes all the devices, methods, skills, and techniques used by the supervisor to keep himself and the employees informed as to their progress toward the objectives they are pursuing. The extent to which the employee has mastered the knowledge, skills, and abilities, or changed his attitudes, as determined by the program objectives, is the extent to which instruction has succeeded or failed.
Evaluation should not be confined to the end of the lesson, day, or program but should be used continuously. We shall note later the way this relates to the rest of the teaching process.

2. Teaching Methods
A teaching method is a pattern of identifiable student and instructor activity used in presenting training material.
All supervisors are faced with the problem of deciding which method should be used at a given time.

a. Lecture
The lecture is direct oral presentation of material by the supervisor. The present trend is to place less emphasis on the trainer's activity and more on that of the trainee.

b. Discussion
Teaching by discussion or conference involves using questions and other techniques to arouse interest and focus attention upon certain areas, and by doing so creating a learning situation. This can be one of the most

valuable methods because it gives the employees an opportunity to express their ideas and pool their knowledge.

c.  Demonstration
The demonstration is used to teach how something works or how to do something. It can be used to show a principle or what the results of a series of actions will be. A well-staged demonstration is particularly effective because it shows proper methods of performance in a realistic manner.

d.  Performance
Performance is one of the most fundamental of all learning techniques or teaching methods. The trainee may be able to tell how a specific operation should be performed but he cannot be sure he knows how to perform the operation until he has done so.
As with all methods, there are certain advantages and disadvantages to each method.

e.  Which Method to Use
Moreover, there are other methods and techniques of teaching. It is difficult to use any method without other methods entering into it. In any learning situation, a combination of methods is usually more effective than any one method alone.

Finally, evaluation must be integrated into the other aspects of the teaching-learning process.

It must be used in the motivation of the trainees; it must be used to assist in developing understanding during the training; and it must be related to employee application of the results of training.

This is distinctly the role of the supervisor.

# HVAC TERMS

Basic Cooling Circuit
Basic cooling is heat-moving - heat absorption. Heat is absorbed when liquid is boiled to a vapor. The temperature at which liquid boils is determined by pressure. Reducing pressure lowers the boiling point, and increasing pressure raises the boiling point. Water boils at 212°F at sea level; higher altitude lowers the boiling point. Boilers use the principle of heating water under pressure to raise the boiling point.

*Simple Cooling Circuit* = enclosed chamber (evaporator), compressor, expansion device, metering device, discharge device, filter-drier sight glass

**Compressor**
Maintains low pressure - reduces pressure on vapor on intake stroke, compresses vapor on compression stroke, discharges vapor under high pressure at outlet.

*Compressors* = Reciprocating piston driven by internally sealed motor or shaft driven by external (open-drive) motor. Hermetically sealed/welded housing; semi-hermetically bolted housing. Seal on the open drive is a disadvantage; it may leak. Small appliance compressors are often the rotary type, hermetically sealed. Residential A/C, refrigeration, hermetic/semi-hermetic rec. piston or scroll type. Large compressors (chillers, cooling plants) rec./screw/centrifugal type. Must cool compressor motor.

**Expansion Device** = expansion valve, capillary tube, fixed restrictor. Small, easily clogged orifices.

*Low Side* = metering device, evaporator, expansion device, and intake (suction) side of compressor. Accumulator traps liquid at outlet of evaporator. Low side pressures are typically under 100 psi.

*High Side* = discharge side of compressor, condenser and liquid line. Receivers to store excess refrigerant at outlet of condenser.

**Filter-Drier**
Filters contaminants, removes moisture. Sight glass in liquid line to view flow. Indicator of proper charge is solid liquid flowing through sight glass.

**Condenser**
High pressure heat transfer coil; accepts high temperature-high pressure gas from compressor, cools and condenses it to a low temperature-high pressure liquid.

**Refrigerant**
Liquid with a boiling point below desired evaporator temperature. For A/C refrigerants a boiling point below 70° F.

*Access* = pinched-off tubes (small), Schrader valves (medium), service valves (large, 3 positions)

*Relief valves* = protect against excessive high pressure. Relief valves cannot be installed in series. Test pressures cannot exceed rating on dataplate.

*Superheated gas* ideal for compressors (no liquid).

## Compressor Lubricants
Long list of requirements. High miscibility (ability to mix with refrigerants). Polyester or "ester" based lubricants. Use alkylbenzenes for ternary blends containing HCFC's. Generally never mix lubricants.

## Leak Detection
System must be sealed for reliability and environment.

## Vacuum Pump
System must be evacuated and dehydrated prior to charging. Contaminants change pressure/temperature relationship and will cause system failure. Acids produced will corrode metal parts, decrease performance, and increase service needs.

## Evacuation Procedure
*Pressure Readings* = relative to a pressure zone.
*Absolute Pressure* = outer space, total vacuum, zero pressure (0 psi Absolute)
*Gauge Pressure* = pressure relative to atmospheric pressure of 14.7 psi.
A gauge calibrated to read absolute pressure reads 14.7 *psia*. When disconnected at sea level, it reads 0 psia in deep space. A gauge calibrated to read gauge pressure reads 0 *psig* when disconnected at sea level and -14.7 psig in space. Gauge readings are more useful in A/C-Refrigeration. Temperature/pressure charts generally use gauge and Fahrenheit values.
*Inches of Mercury* (in Hg) are used for pressures below atmospheric; always gauge readings.
*Microns of Mercury* = 500 micron vacuum is adequate for more refrigerant circuit evacuations.

### Manifold Gauge Set
Used for preliminary leak checking, evacuation, charging and refrigerant transfer.
Consists of a pair of gauges and a manifold chamber.
Low pressure gauge on left and blue; high pressure gauge on right and red.
Three sections of manifold chamber: Low side (left), high side (right) and center hose flow control.
Center service hose connected to external equipment needed for specific job (evacuation, charging, recovery, etc.)
Opening hand valve opens chamber to pressure of center chamber. Both valves open all three chambers at same pressure.

www.ingramcontent.com/pod-product-compliance
Lightning Source LLC
Chambersburg PA
CBHW081825300426
44116CB00014B/2484